# Learning Cocos2d-JS Game Development

Learn to create robust and engaging cross-platform HTML5 games using Cocos2d-JS

**Emanuele Feronato**

**[PACKT]** **open source**
PUBLISHING      community experience distilled

BIRMINGHAM - MUMBAI

# Learning Cocos2d-JS Game Development

First published: January 2015

Production reference: 1070115

Published by Packt Publishing Ltd.
Livery Place
35 Livery Street
Birmingham B3 2PB, UK.

ISBN 978-1-78439-007-5

www.packtpub.com

# Credits

**Author**
Emanuele Feronato

**Reviewers**
Pradyumna Doddala
Pavel Goodanets
Marc Estruch Tena
Jialong Zhai

**Commissioning Editor**
Ashwin Nair

**Acquisition Editor**
James Jones

**Content Development Editor**
Samantha Gonsalves

**Technical Editor**
Parag Topre

**Copy Editor**
Relin Hedly

**Project Coordinator**
Sanchita Mandal

**Proofreaders**
Simran Bhogal
Stephen Copestake
Maria Gould
Ameesha Green
Paul Hindle

**Indexer**
Rekha Nair

**Production Coordinator**
Alwin Roy

**Cover Work**
Alwin Roy

# Foreword

Known by developers all over the world, Cocos2d-x has always endeavored to help developers build and port their games on iOS, Android, and many more native platforms. However, not many developers are aware that the Cocos2d-x team also provides an efficient game engine called Cocos2d-JS to assist users developing cross-native and web platform games with only one code base.

The year 2014 has certainly been a big year for Cocos2d-JS. It became more widely adopted by big companies all over the world; we've released a major version—3.0—and combined Cocos2d-html5 and Cocos2d-x JSB (JavaScript Binding) into Cocos2d-JS. It supplies your game with cross-browser and cross-platform capabilities accompanied by complete Cocos2d-x features, complete tool chain support, and simple friendly APIs. Furthermore, we reinvented the workflow for all platforms, providing a consistent development experience for whichever platform you want to distribute it to. As a result, the *Code once, run everywhere* principle is easily achieved and feels natural in Cocos2d-JS. With one single JavaScript code base, you can run your game on all web browsers and native platforms, including Mac OS, Windows, iOS, and Android. This will allow your game to deliver in almost all channels of distribution for better opportunities.

Today, I'm more than grateful to witness the creation of this extraordinary book. I believe this book will help us by building a bridge to our developers around the world so they can step over the language barrier. I'd love to express my special thanks to dear Feronato, the author of this amazing book. He started programming when I was a little child in diapers and he's still going strong, inspiring thousands of indie developers around the world—that's surely something!

In this book, Feronato gathered and generously shared with us his profound knowledge in game programming and Cocos2d-JS; he also included a rich collection of examples in each chapter; this, in my opinion, is one of the best ways to help learning, as readers will get a clear sense of how to apply text in the book to real work.

Here, allow me to express my honestly sincere gratitude to Emanuele Feronato for completing such an amazing book.

Hope you all enjoy this amazing book and benefit from it.

**Shun Lin**
Cofounder of Cocos2d-x

# Foreword

As we look forward to 2015 with excitement, I wanted to look back at what we built in 2014 and share with you how important the release of this great book is to our community.

2014 has been an extraordinary year for Cocos2d-JS. Since we announced Cocos2d-JS v3.0 alpha at our spring developers conference in March, we have put our best efforts into building a great and unique game engine for our community. Our mission is to offer an easy *code once, runs everywhere* game development experience and lower the development threshold to bring more developers into the game industry.

Although the version was v3.0, it was the first version of Cocos2d-JS that was inherited from Cocos2d-html5 2.2.3. It has been an entirely new era in Cocos2d's JavaScript development since v3.0; here are the most important things that we have done:

- Combined the Cocos2d-html5 web engine and the native Cocos2d-x JavaScript Bindings engine so that Cocos2d-JS games are equipped naturally with cross-browser and cross-platform abilities.

- Provided a consistent workflow for all platforms — a best ever *Code once, runs everywhere* experience.

- Made a great step forward in performance for both the web engine and native engine.

- Built a bunch of new features such as Facebook Integration, Assets Manager, Object Pool, JS to Objective-C/JAVA reflection, and so on.

As a result, we have started to see many games released with Cocos2d-JS, especially on the Web, iOS, and Android. Today, I'm very proud to witness the very first English book on Cocos2d-JS; it really means a lot to us. Thanks to the great work of Emanuele on this book, I believe it will help many developers all around the world learn not only about Cocos2d-JS, but also game development in general. I'm also convinced that many developers, like you, our dear reader, will enter the game industry because of this book and start a great adventure with your code.

I recommend this book not only because it's the first one, but also because reading this book is a great approach to learning Cocos2d-JS. Emanuele covered all essential parts of Cocos2d-JS in this book; most importantly, he discussed all these topics with rich examples and sample codes. Furthermore, he managed to structure these examples into small games so that readers can progressively see their work turning into real games. I believe this will be a very strong motivation and will bring much fun while learning.

Again, I want to express my appreciation to Emanuele Feronato and this wonderful book. Hope you enjoy learning Cocos2d-JS with Emanuele and enjoy coding games.

**Huabin LING**
Lead Programmer of Cocos2d-JS

# About the Author

**Emanuele Feronato** has been studying programming languages since the early 1980s, with a particular interest in game development. He has taught online programming for European Social Fund (ESF), and then founded a web development company in Italy.

As a game developer, Emanuele developed Flash games sponsored by the biggest game portals and his games have been played more than 90 million times. He now ports most of them on mobile platforms and develops HTML5 games, which have been featured in the most important mobile web markets, such as Amazon.

As a writer, he has worked as a technical reviewer for Packt Publishing and published the books *Flash Game Development by Example* and *Box2D for Flash Games*.

His blog, www.emanueleferonato.com, is one of the most visited blogs about indie game development.

First, I would like to thank Packt Publishing for giving me the opportunity to write this book, especially Richard Harvey, Azharuddin Sheikh, and Samantha Gonsalves for helping me improve the book quality.

The biggest thank you obviously goes to my blog readers and my Facebook fans for appreciating my work, giving me the will to write more and more. Also, thank you for playing my games. Hope you enjoy playing them as much as I enjoyed developing them.

Finally, a special thank you to my wife, Kirenia, for her patience while I was writing the book.

# About the Reviewers

**Pradyumna Doddala** is a passionate technologist and entrepreneur; he is the CEO of Kronch IT and has been an advisor for a couple of technological startups. Pradyumna has focused on different domains, such as augmented reality, life sciences, location-based marketing, and crowdsourcing solutions. He wrote several open source libraries and blog posts to assist his fellow developers. Pradyumna is also a musician and likes to spend his spare time creating music on his guitar.

He is currently working on *Mastering Android UI Development*, *Packt Publishing*.

I want to thank my mom and the publishers for all the support.

**Pavel Goodanets** is a programmer, writer, and game designer from Latvia. He loves point-and-click adventures, games with strong narratives, and experimental forms of gameplay. Pavel speaks Russian and English. His website is `http://pavel-insight.com` and you can contact him at `pavel.insight@gmail.com`.

**Marc Estruch Tena** has completed his BS degree in Multimedia Engineering with honors from La Salle — Ramon LLull University, Barcelona, Spain, in 2012. Since then, he has been employed as a research associate at the Human Sensing Laboratory in the Robotics Institute of Carnegie Mellon University, Pittsburgh, PA, USA.

As a member of this research laboratory, he has developed several applications and games for web and mobile platforms using Computer Vision algorithms that feature the IntraFace (`http://humansensing.cs.cmu.edu/intraface`) software for facial image analysis. His interest in Human-computer Interaction and his programming and design skills have led him to pursue new ways of user interaction with different tools and frameworks.

**Jialong Zhai** pursued a post-graduate degree in Computer Science from Xidian University. He has lots of experience in mobile and web games development and is good at C++ and JavaScript. Currently, Jialong works for the Cocos engine team, bringing free open source game engines to people.

First, I must thank the author and the staff of Packt Publishing, Sanchita and Samantha. This book is the result of their hard work. Secondly, I would like to thank my coworkers Shun, Dingping, and Huabin; they gave me many good suggestions during the reviewing process.

# www.PacktPub.com

## Support files, eBooks, discount offers, and more

For support files and downloads related to your book, please visit www.PacktPub.com.

Did you know that Packt offers eBook versions of every book published, with PDF and ePub files available? You can upgrade to the eBook version at www.PacktPub.com and, as a print book customer, you are entitled to a discount on the eBook copy. Get in touch with us at service@packtpub.com for more details.

At www.PacktPub.com, you can also read a collection of free technical articles, sign up for a range of free newsletters, and receive exclusive discounts and offers on Packt books and eBooks.

https://www2.packtpub.com/books/subscription/packtlib

Do you need instant solutions to your IT questions? PacktLib is Packt's online digital book library. Here, you can search, access, and read Packt's entire library of books.

## Why subscribe?

- Fully searchable across every book published by Packt
- Copy-and-paste, print, and bookmark content
- On-demand and accessible via a web browser

## Free access for Packt account holders

If you have an account with Packt at www.PacktPub.com, you can use this to access PacktLib today and view 9 entirely free books. Simply use your login credentials for immediate access.

*I want to dedicate this book to my little daughter Kimora. At the moment she's playing my games and she's my favourite beta tester.*

*I love you "Cindy Sindientes".*

# Table of Contents

Preface                                                              1

Chapter 1: Hello World – A Cross-platform Game                       7
  Why should I make cross-platform games?                   8
  What Cocos2d-JS is and how it works                        8
    Requirements to run Cocos2d-JS                  8
  The structure of your Cocos2d-JS project                  10
  Hello Cross-World                                         11
  Preloading and adding images                              14
  Removing images and changing the background color         18
  Summary                                                   19

Chapter 2: Adding Interactivity – The Making of a
Concentration Game                                                   21
  Creating multiple instances of game assets               22
  Adding a gradient background                              24
  Extending the Sprite class beyond its capabilities       25
  Making assets react to clicks and touches                27
    Picking a tile as an initial attempt          27
  Changing sprite images on the fly                        30
    Showing the tile picture                      30
  Shuffling the tiles and adding the score                 34
  Summary                                                   36

Chapter 3: Moving Sprites Around the Screen –
An Endless Runner                                                    37
  Loading and placing graphic resources                    38
  Adding the endless scrolling background                  39
  Adding the spaceship                                     42
  Controlling an spaceship                                 44

| | |
|---|---|
| Adding asteroids | 47 |
| Asteroid versus spaceship collision | 50 |
| Invulnerability | 52 |
| Preventing the spaceship from flying off the screen | 53 |
| Adding particles | 54 |
| Summary | 56 |
| **Chapter 4: Learn about Swipes through the making of Sokoban** | **57** |
| Loading graphic assets | 58 |
| Building a level | 61 |
| Detecting swipes | 66 |
| Completing the game | 70 |
| Summary | 72 |
| **Chapter 5: Become a Musical Maestro** | **73** |
| Choosing sounds | 73 |
| Preloading sounds | 74 |
| Creating a sound menu | 75 |
| Managing music and sound effects | 77 |
| Summary | 79 |
| **Chapter 6: Controlling the Game with Virtual Pads** | **81** |
| Overview of virtual pads | 82 |
| First things first – the game | 85 |
| Controlling the cart with ghost buttons | 90 |
| Controlling the cart with a virtual pad | 93 |
| Controlling the cart just with your finger | 97 |
| Summary | 99 |
| **Chapter 7: Adding Physics to Your Games Using the Box2D Engine** | **101** |
| Before you start | 102 |
| Adding the Box2D engine to your project | 102 |
| Configuring the physics world | 104 |
| Adding bodies to the world | 107 |
| Updating sprite position as the world changes | 113 |
| Selecting and destroying world bodies | 116 |
| Checking for collisions among bodies | 118 |
| Summary | 119 |

**Chapter 8: Adding Physics to Your Games Using the Chipmunk2D Engine** — **121**

**Adding the Chipmunk2D engine to your project** — **122**
A physics game, without physics — 122
**Configuring the physics space** — **124**
**Adding bodies to the space** — **125**
Updating Chipmunk2D space and using debug draw — 127
**Selecting and destroying space bodies** — **129**
**Checking for collisions among bodies** — **132**
**Using your own graphic assets** — **134**
**Summary** — **136**

**Chapter 9: Creating Your Own Blockbuster Game – A Complete Match 3 Game** — **137**

**Setting up the game** — **138**
Creating the board — 139
Selecting and deselecting the first globe — 142
Making globez chains — 146
Backtracking — 148
Removing globez — 149
Making the globez fall down — 151
Creating new globez — 154
Bonus – using the drawing API for a visual feedback — 155
**Where to go now** — **158**
Protect your code — 158
Port your game on mobile devices as a native app — 159
Publishing your game — 159
Licensing your game — 160
Staying up-to-date — 160
**Summary** — **160**

**Index** — **161**

# Preface

Mobile HTML5 casual games are experiencing a golden age these days. Not only famous Flash hits and successful native mobile games, but also original games tailored for mobile browsers are played by millions of players everyday.

With a continuously growing number of mobile devices available to play HTML5 games, and with each one having its own resolution, and display size, and ratio, creating a game version for each device would make you waste a lot of time. That's why there's a new way to make HTML5 games called **cross-platform**. It means you create a game once, and some magic adapts it to every device capable of running HTML5 content.

This magic is called **Cocos2d-JS**, which allows you to focus on what you actually love, making games, and takes care of screen resolutions and ratios. Also, you will be using one of the simplest and most widely known languages ever: JavaScript. Last but not least, it's free. You can create the next big game at no cost.

Throughout this book, you will learn how to make games using Cocos2d-JS in the most fun and productive way. We know you hate boring theories, so we did our best to focus the entire book on one single word: action.

Learn Cocos2d-JS with examples taken from the most successful game genres; see how easy it is to create a game once, and then make it run on each device.

# What this book covers

*Chapter 1, Hello World – A Cross-platform Game*, will show you how to create a blueprint that you will be using for every game you will make with Cocos2d-JS. This chapter will also guide you through the creation of an environment to create and test your cross-platform games.

*Chapter 2, Adding Interactivity – The Making of a Concentration Game*, guides you through the creation of one of the most popular games that makes you learn how to create sprites and interact with them both with the mouse and finger.

*Chapter 3, Moving Sprites Around the Screen – An Endless Runner*, introduces scrolling and sprite movements using motion tweens in the creation of a space-themed endless runner. Particle effects and collision detection complete the game experience.

*Chapter 4, Learn about Swipes through the making of Sokoban*, shows you how to create a classic puzzle game that you can control with the most intuitive way used these days: swiping on the game.

*Chapter 5, Become a Musical Maestro*, examines the importance of having sound effects and background music in your games. This chapter also shows you how to start and stop sounds and loops by adjusting their volume.

*Chapter 6, Controlling the Game with Virtual Pads*, provides you three different ways to control your games with virtual pads when you build a fruit game. Virtual buttons and analogic pads will be your best friends when you create your next game.

*Chapter 7, Adding Physics to Your Games Using the Box2D Engine*, shows you the magic of physics engines in the creation of the blockbuster Totem Destroyer game, which you will easily build using the Box2D physics engine. You will also learn how to create, destroy, skin, and interact with physics bodies in a realistic physics environment.

*Chapter 8, Adding Physics to Your Games Using the Chipmunk2D Engine*, creates the same Totem Destroyer game, this time using Chipmunk2D rather than Box2D. While the Web is divided by the *Box2D versus Chipmunk2D* war, you will learn both of them, leaving the choice of your favorite physics engine up to you.

*Chapter 9, Creating Your Own Blockbuster Game – A Complete Match 3 Game*, completes the book with the creation of the most successful game genre today: a Match-3 game. At the end of the chapter, you will also find some hints and suggestions on protecting, promoting, marketing, and monetizing your game.

# What you need for this book

Cocos2d-JS is so easy to use, apart being free; it basically does not require anything but a text editor and a server to run your projects. If you want, you can use the Cocos2d-JS official IDE, but you're welcome to use your favorite text editor if you prefer.

# Who this book is for

Whether you are an experienced game developer coming from another language or a complete novice, this book can guide you through the creation of cross-platform games. Some basic knowledge of JavaScript is recommended, then just follow book examples.

# Conventions

In this book, you will find a number of styles of text that distinguish between different kinds of information. Here are some examples of these styles, and an explanation of their meaning.

Code words in text, database table names, folder names, filenames, file extensions, pathnames, dummy URLs, user input, and Twitter handles are shown as follows: "I found myself almost rewriting the game with a series of if.. then.. else trying to make it look good on any device."

A block of code is set as follows:

```
var gameScene = cc.Scene.extend({
  onEnter:function () {
    this._super();
    gameLayer = new game();
    gameLayer.init();
    this.addChild(gameLayer);
  }
});
```

When we wish to draw your attention to a particular part of a code block, the relevant lines or items are set in bold:

```
var gameScene = cc.Scene.extend({
  onEnter:function () {
    this._super();
    gameLayer = new game();
    gameLayer.init();
    this.addChild(gameLayer);
  }
});
```

**New terms** and **important words** are shown in bold. Words that you see on the screen, in menus or dialog boxes for example, appear in the text like this: "If you now open the developer console, you should see: **my awesome game starts here**".

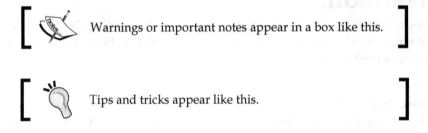

> Warnings or important notes appear in a box like this.

> Tips and tricks appear like this.

# Reader feedback

Feedback from our readers is always welcome. Let us know what you think about this book—what you liked or may have disliked. Reader feedback is important for us to develop titles that you really get the most out of.

To send us general feedback, simply send an e-mail to feedback@packtpub.com, and mention the book title via the subject of your message.

If there is a topic that you have expertise in and you are interested in either writing or contributing to a book, see our author guide on www.packtpub.com/authors.

# Customer support

Now that you are the proud owner of a Packt book, we have a number of things to help you to get the most from your purchase.

# Downloading the example code

You can download the example code files for all Packt books you have purchased from your account at `http://www.packtpub.com`. If you purchased this book elsewhere, you can visit `http://www.packtpub.com/support` and register to have the files e-mailed directly to you.

# Downloading the color images of this book

We also provide you with a PDF fie that has color images of the screenshots/ diagrams used in this book. The color images will help you better understand the changes in the output. You can download this fie from: `https://www.packtpub.com/sites/default/files/downloads/0075OS_ColoredImages.pdf`

# Errata

Although we have taken every care to ensure the accuracy of our content, mistakes do happen. If you find a mistake in one of our books — maybe a mistake in the text or the code — we would be grateful if you would report this to us. By doing so, you can save other readers from frustration and help us improve subsequent versions of this book. If you find any errata, please report them by visiting `http://www.packtpub.com/submit-errata`, selecting your book, clicking on the **errata submission form** link, and entering the details of your errata. Once your errata are verified, your submission will be accepted and the errata will be uploaded on our website, or added to any list of existing errata, under the Errata section of that title. Any existing errata can be viewed by selecting your title from `http://www.packtpub.com/support`.

# Piracy

Piracy of copyright material on the Internet is an ongoing problem across all media. At Packt, we take the protection of our copyright and licenses very seriously. If you come across any illegal copies of our works, in any form, on the Internet, please provide us with the location address or website name immediately so that we can pursue a remedy.

Please contact us at copyright@packtpub.com with a link to the suspected pirated material.

We appreciate your help in protecting our authors, and our ability to bring you valuable content.

# Questions

You can contact us at questions@packtpub.com if you are having a problem with any aspect of the book, and we will do our best to address it.

# 1
# Hello World – A Cross-platform Game

The legend says that the first working script you should do when learning a new language is the classic Hello World printed somewhere on the screen.

This chapter will guide you through the creation of a cross-platform Hello World example, covering these concepts:

- The theory behind the creation of cross platform games
- Cocos2d-JS installation and setup
- A Cocos2d-JS project blueprint
- Scenes, Layers, and Sprites
- Preloading images
- Adding images
- Removing images

By the end of the chapter, you will be able to create a template project to create any kind of Cocos2d-JS cross-platform game that is capable of running on various devices at different resolutions.

# Why should I make cross-platform games?

This is a very important question. I asked it to myself a lot of times when HTML5 mobile gaming started to become popular. I was just thinking it was a waste of time to simply care about the different screen resolutions and aspect ratios, so my first HTML5 game was made to perfectly fit my iPad 2 tablet.

When I finally showed it to sponsors, most of them said something like "Hey, I like the game, but unfortunately it does not look that good on my iPhone". "Don't worry", I said, "you'll get the game optimized for iPad and iPhone". Unfortunately, it did not look that good on the Galaxy Note. Neither did it on the Samsung S4.

You can imagine the rest of this story. I found myself almost rewriting the game with a series of `if.. then.. else` loops, trying to make it look good on any device.

This is why you should make a cross-platform game: *To code once and rule them all*. Focus on game development and let a framework do the dirty work for you.

# What Cocos2d-JS is and how it works

**Cocos2d-JS** is a free open source 2D game framework. It can help you to develop cross-platform browser games and native applications. This framework allows you to write games in JavaScript. So, if you have already developed JavaScript applications, you don't have to learn a new language from scratch. Throughout this book, you will learn how to create almost any kind of cross-platform game using a familiar and intuitive language.

# Requirements to run Cocos2d-JS

Before you start, let's see what software you need to install on your computer in order to start developing with Cocos2d-JS:

- Firstly, you need a text editor. The official IDE for Cocos2d-JS coding is **Cocos Code IDE**, which you can download for free at `http://www.cocos2d-x.org/products/codeide`. It features auto completion, code hinting, and some more interesting characteristics to speed up your coding. If you are used to your favorite code editor, that's fine. There are plenty of them, but I personally use PSPad (you can find this at `http://www.pspad.com/`) on my Windows machine and TextWrangler (you can find this at `http://www.barebones.com/products/textwrangler/`) on the Mac. They are both free and easy to use, so you can download and have them installed in a matter of minutes.

- To test your Cocos2d-JS projects, you will need to install a web server on your computer to override security limits when running your project locally. I am using WAMP (`http://www.wampserver.com/`) on my Windows machine, and MAMP (`http://www.mamp.info/`) on the Mac.

 Again, both are free to use as you won't need the PRO version, which is also available for Mac computers. Explaining all the theory behind this is beyond the scope of this book, but you can find all the required information as well as the installation documentation on the official sites.

- If you prefer, you can test your projects directly online by uploading them on an FTP space you own and call them directly from the web. In this case, you don't need to have a web server installed on your computer, but I highly recommend using WAMP or MAMP instead.

- I personally use Google Chrome as the default browser to test my projects. As these projects are meant to be cross-platform games, it should run in the same way on every browser, so feel free to use the browser you prefer.

The latest information about Cocos2d-JS can be found on the official page `http://www.cocos2d-x.org/wiki/Cocos2d-JS`, while the latest version can be downloaded at `http://www.cocos2d-x.org/download`.

 Cocos2d-JS is updated quite frequently, but at the time of writing, the latest stable release is v3.1. Although new releases always bring some changes, all examples included in this book should work fine with any release marked as 3.x as there aren't huge changes in the roadmap.

You will notice the download file is a `ZIP` file that is greater than 250 MB. Don't worry. Most of the content of the package is made by docs, graphic assets, and examples, while the only required folder, at the moment, is the one called `cocos2d-html5`.

# The structure of your Cocos2d-JS project

Every HTML5 game is basically a web page with some magic in it; this is what you are going to create with Cocos2d-JS: a web page with some magic in it.

To perform this magic, a certain file structure needs to be created, so let's take a look at a screenshot of a folder with a Cocos2d-JS project in it:

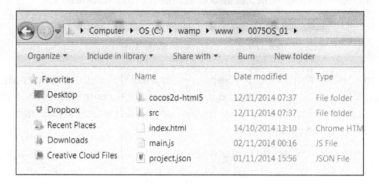

This is what you are going to build; to tell you the truth, this is a picture of the actual project folder I built for the example to be explained in this chapter, which is placed in the WAMP `localhost` folder on my computer. It couldn't be any more real.

So, let's take a look at the files to be created:

- `cocos2d-html5`: This is the folder you will find in the zip archive.
- `index.html`: This is the web page that will contain the game.
- `main.js`:This is a file required by Cocos2d-JS with the Cocos2d-JS function calls to make the game start. You will create this within the next few minutes.
- `project.json`: This is a **JavaScript Object Notation (JSON)** with some basic configurations. This is what you need to make your game run. Well, almost, because the actual game will be placed in the `src` folder. Let's see a few other things first.

# Hello Cross-World

The time has come, the boring theory has ended, and we can now start coding our first project. Let's begin!

1. Firstly, create a page called `index.html` in the root of the game folder and write this HTML code:

```
<!DOCTYPE html>
  <head>
    <title>
      My Awesome game
    </title>
    <script src="cocos2d-html5/CCBoot.js" type="text/javascript">
</script>
    <script src="main.js" type="text/javascript">
</script>
  </head>
  <body style="padding:0;margin:0;background-color:#000000;">
  </body>
</html>
```

There's nothing interesting in it as it is just plain HTML. Let's take a closer look at these lines to see what is going on:

```
<script src=" cocos2d-html5/CCBoot.js "></script>
```

Here, I am including the Cocos2d-JS boot file to make the framework start:

```
<script src="main.js"></script>
```

From the preceding line, this is where we call the script with the actual game we are going to build. Next, we have the following code:

```
<canvas id="gameCanvas"></canvas>
```

This is the canvas we will use to display the game. Notice here that the canvas does not have a width and height, as they will be defined by the game itself.

2. Next is the creation of `main.js`: the only file we will call from our main `index.html` page. This is more of a configuration file rather than the game itself, so you won't code anything that is game-related at the moment. However, the file you are going to build will be the blueprint you will be using in all your Cocos2d-JS games.

The content of `main.js` is as follows:

```
cc.game.onStart = function(){
    cc.view.setDesignResolutionSize(320, 480, cc.ResolutionPolicy.
SHOW_ALL);
    cc.director.runScene(new gameScene());
};
cc.game.run();
```

Don't worry about the code at the moment; it looks a lot more complicated than it really is. At the moment, the only line we have to worry about is the one that defines the resolution policy.

 One of the most challenging tasks in cross-platform development is to provide a good gaming experience, no matter what browser or what device the game is running on. However, the problem here is that each device has its own resolution, screen size, and ratio.

Cocos2d-JS allows us to handle different resolutions in a similar way web designers do when building responsive design. At the moment, we just want to adapt the game canvas to fit the browser window while targeting the most popular resolution, which is 320x480 (portrait mode). That's what this line does:

```
 cc.view.setDesignResolutionSize(320, 480, cc.ResolutionPolicy.
SHOW_ALL);
```

Using these settings, you should be pretty sure that your game will run on every device, although you will be working in a low resolution.

Also, have a look at this line:

```
cc.director.runScene(new gameScene());
```

Basically, a Cocos2d-JS game is made by a scene where the game itself runs. There can be more scenes in the same game. Imagine a scene with the title screen, a scene with the game over screen, and a scene with the game itself. At the moment, you only have one scene called `gameScene`. Remember this name because you are going to use it later.

3. Following this, the next required blueprint file you are going to build is `project.json`, which has some interesting settings. Let's take a look at the file first:

```json
{
  "debugMode" : 0,
  "showFPS" : false,
  "frameRate" : 60,
  "id" : "gameCanvas",
  "renderMode" : 0,
  "engineDir":"cocos2d-html5/",

  "modules" : ["cocos2d"],

  "jsList" : [
    "src/gamescript.js"
  ]
}
```

What do these lines mean? Let's see them one by one:

- ° `debugMode`: This is the object key that determines the level of debug warnings. It has a range from 0 to 6. Leave it at 0 at the moment since the project is very simple and we won't make any errors.
- ° `showFPS`: This object can be **true** or **false**; it shows or hides the FPS meter on the screen.
- ° `frameRate`: This object sets the frame rate of your game. Set it to `60` to have a smooth game.
- ° `id`: This is the DOM element that is required to run the game. Do you remember you gave your canvas the `gameCanvas` id? Here you are.
- ° `engineDir`: This is the folder where Cocos2d-JS is installed.
- ° `modules`: This object engines the modules to load. At the moment, we only need the basic Cocos2d library.
- ° `jsList`: This is an array with the files used in the game. This means we are going to create our game in `src/gamescript.js`.

4. Finally, we arrive at the game script itself. This is the one that will contain the actual game, `gamescript.js`, which at the moment is just a plain declaration of the game scene:

```javascript
var gameScene = cc.Scene.extend({
  onEnter:function () {
    this._super();
```

```
        console.log("my awesome game starts here");
    }
});
```

Here, you want to save everything and call `index.html` page from your `localhost` (refer to your WAMP or MAMP docs) in your browser. If you now open the developer console, you should see:

**my awesome game starts here**

Congratulations! This means you have successfully managed to create a Cocos2d-JS template file to build your future games.

Let's build our first mini game at once!

# Preloading and adding images

In this example, I am using a 64x64 PNG image representing a target, as shown in the following figure:

You are obviously free to use whatever image you prefer.

When you load a web page, in most cases, the page is loaded and shown before all images are loaded. This might sound okay on a web page because readers won't mind if they have to wait a couple of seconds before an image is showed, but this definitely can't happen in a game. This means our images need to be preloaded, and Cocos2d-JS can easily handle this. The steps on how to preload images in your game are as follows:

1. This is the first time you add this line to the `project.json` file:

    ```
    {
        "debugMode" : 0,
        "showFPS" : false,
        "frameRate" : 60,
        "id" : "gameCanvas",
        "renderMode" : 0,
    ```

```
    "engineDir":"cocos2d-html5/",

    "modules" : ["cocos2d"],

    "jsList" : [
      "src/loadassets.js",
      "src/gamescript.js"
    ]
}
```

This means you are going to create another file called `loadassets.js` in the same `src` folder where you just created `gamescript.js`.

This is the content of `loadassets.js`:

```
var gameResources = [
    "assets/target.png"
];
```

An array called `gameResources` stores the assets to preload. So, you should create a folder called `assets` and place the `target.png` image inside this folder.

 To keep the project organization clear, I am going to place all game assets in a folder called `assets`.

2.  Now that Cocos2d-JS is aware which images need to be preloaded, we only need to tell the game that it has to preload them before the scene starts, so we need to add a couple of lines to `main.js`:

```
cc.game.onStart = function(){
  cc.view.setDesignResolutionSize(320, 480, cc.ResolutionPolicy.
SHOW_ALL);
  cc.LoaderScene.preload(gameResources, function () {
    cc.director.runScene(new gameScene());
  }, this);
};
cc.game.run();
```

The `cc.LoaderScene.preload` constructor will preload scene resources taken from the `gameResources` array defined in `loadassets.js`. All puzzle pieces match perfectly.

3.  Finally, let's add the target to the game by rewriting the `gamescript.js` file:

```
var gameScene = cc.Scene.extend({
  onEnter:function () {
  this._super();
    var gameLayer = new game();
    gameLayer.init();
    this.addChild(gameLayer);
  }
});
var game = cc.Layer.extend({
  init:function () {
    this._super();
    var target = cc.Sprite.create("assets/target.png");
    this.addChild(target,0);
  }
});
```

If you developed Flash games using **AS3** (**ActionScript 3**), you will find Cocos2d-JS assets hierarchy familiar to display objects. If you are new to this, allow me to explain what happens:

1.  Like all frameworks that deal with graphic resources, Cocos2d-JS has hierarchy rules. On the top of such a hierarchy, we find the `Scene` object. Each scene contains some game logic; think about a main menu scene, a game scene, and a game over scene.

2.  Each scene contains one or more `Layer` objects; layers define which content should be at the top of other content. In a real-world example, a level background is in the bottom-most layer, player and enemies will be created in a layer above the background, and game information such as score and remaining lives are placed on the topmost layer.

3.  Finally, all layers can have one or more `Sprite` objects, which are the graphic assets themselves such as the player, the enemies, or in this case, the target.

4.  To summarize, the code means that once `gameScene` is executed, create and add the `game` layer, and in this layer, add the `target` sprite.

It's time to test the project by calling the `index.html` file, and the following screenshot is what you should get:

Although it's just a basic project, there are several things to take note of:

- Images are preloaded and a default loading screen is shown. This means the preloader works.
- Although our project is set to work at 320x480, the game stretches to fill the browser completely, thanks to the resolution policy set before.
- Images have their registration point in the center of the image, whereas most frameworks have their image registration point in the upper-left corner.
- The origin (0,0) of the scene takes place in the lower-left corner, while most frameworks have their origin in the upper-left corner.

To top it all, you were able to create your first project. To change the target position and place it in the middle of the screen, just use the `setPosition` method that changes `gamescript.js` this way:

```
var gameScene = cc.Scene.extend({
  onEnter:function () {
  this._super();
    var gameLayer = new game();
    gameLayer.init();
```

```
      this.addChild(gameLayer);
    }
});

var game = cc.Layer.extend({
  init:function () {
    this._super();
    var target = cc.Sprite.create("assets/target.png");
    this.addChild(target,0);
    target.setPosition(160,240);
  }
});
```

Test the project and you will see the target image in the middle of the screen.

# Removing images and changing the background color

Now you know how to add images you might also be interested in knowing how to remove them. It's really intuitive: you added images with the addChild method, so you are going to remove them with the removeChild method.

Moreover, we will change the background color by adding an actual background layer, which covers the entire scene with a solid color.

There are just a couple of lines to add to gamescript.js:

```
var gameScene = cc.Scene.extend({
  onEnter:function () {
  this._super();
    var gameLayer = new game();
    gameLayer.init();
    this.addChild(gameLayer);
  }
});
var backgroundLayer;
var game = cc.Layer.extend({
  init:function () {
    this._super();
    backgroundLayer = cc.LayerColor.create(new cc.Color(40,40,40,255),
320, 480);
this.addChild(backgroundLayer);
```

```
    var target = cc.Sprite.create("assets/target.png");
    backgroundLayer.addChild(target,0);
    target.setPosition(160,240);
  setTimeout(function(){
    backgroundLayer.removeChild(target);
    }, 3000);
  }
});
```

In the preceding code, backgroundLayer is a new layer that will be filled with a new color with the **RGBA** format (in this case, a full opaque dark grey), which will also contain the target image.

After three seconds since its creation, the target is removed from backgroundLayer with the removeChild method.

# Summary

In this chapter, you learned how to install, configure, and run your first Cocos2d-JS project. You also learned how to place images on the screen.

Placing more instances of the same object will be one of the topics covered in the next chapter, where you will also create your first game, so no looking yet!

Test yourself with an exercise by trying to put 10 targets on the screen at random positions.

# 2
# Adding Interactivity – The Making of a Concentration Game

By definition, a game is interactive in some way. Players have to be *part* of it by doing things. The simplest form of interactivity is clicking or touching tiles in the game.

A Concentration game is simple to explain, but it will cover some new and important concepts, such as:

- Creating multiple instances of game assets
- Extending classes to improve its capabilities. Actually, there are no classes in JavaScript, but they are emulated using variables and prototypes
- Adding gradients
- Making assets react to clicks and touches
- Changing sprite images on the fly
- Adding text labels
- Removing sprites from the game

By the end of the chapter, you will be able to create a full Concentration game using space for customization.

As the project created in the previous chapter is more than just a Hello World game and rather acts as a blueprint for all your future projects, you'll start building our Concentration game out of the previously finished project.

# Creating multiple instances of game assets

The first thing you have to do in the making of a Concentration game is draw the tiles that you will use in the game. Here are the pictures used for the covered tiles and the eight different tiles that could be potentially matched, all saved in the assets folder, as explained in the previous chapter:

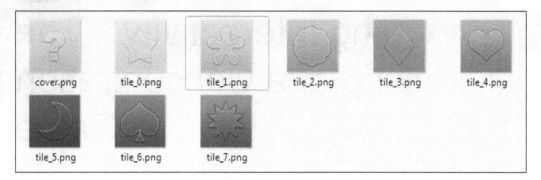

Each tile is a 64 x 64 PNG file, where the covered tile is called cover.png, while the tile to be matched is named with a progressive number from 0 to 7: **tile_0**, **tile_1**, until **tile_7**. This is because the actual board tile values will be stored in an array whose values will range from 0 to 7, and it will be easy to assign value 0 to **tile_0**, value 1 to **tile_1**, and so on.

With these nine files in the assets folder, you are ready to load them, thanks to the loadassets.js file located in the src folder of our project:

```
var gameResources = ["assets/cover.png",
  "assets/tile_0.png",
  "assets/tile_1.png",
  "assets/tile_2.png",
  "assets/tile_3.png",
  "assets/tile_4.png",
  "assets/tile_5.png",
  "assets/tile_6.png",
  "assets/tile_7.png"
];
```

The images are loaded in the same way as in the previous chapter; you then place all the 16 covered tiles.

This is the content of `gamescript.js`, which is basically the same you used in the previous chapter, except sprite creation is inside a `for` loop that will be executed 16 times:

```
var gameScene = cc.Scene.extend({
  onEnter:function () {
    this._super();
    gameLayer = new game();
    gameLayer.init();
    this.addChild(gameLayer);
  }
});

var game = cc.Layer.extend({
  init:function () {
    this._super();
    for(i=0;i<16;i++){
      var tile = cc.Sprite.create("assets/cover.png");
      this.addChild(tile,0);
      tile.setPosition(49+i%4*74,400-Math.floor(i/4)*74);
    }
  }
});
```

The strange numbers in the `setPosition` method places the group of 64 x 64 tiles in a 4 x 4 grid on the stage. You can use some math to change the tiles' position the way you prefer.

Test the game and this is what you will see on the screen:

This is a nice grid of covered tiles, but the background is poor. It's time to work on it a bit more.

# Adding a gradient background

A quick and easy way to improve the background is to add a gradient. Most of the skies and sceneries you see in the background of your favorite games are just gradients.

You are going to add a gradient layer conveniently called `gradient` to the game simply by adding these two lines to `gamescript.js`:

```
var gameScene = cc.Scene.extend({
  // same as before
});

var game = cc.Layer.extend({
  init:function () {
    this._super();
    var gradient = cc.LayerGradient.create(cc.color(0,0,0,255),
cc.color(0x46,0x82,0xB4,255));
    this.addChild(gradient);
    for(i=0;i<16;i++){
      var tile = cc.Sprite.create("assets/cover.png");
      this.addChild(tile,0);
      tile.setPosition(49+i%4*74,400-Math.floor(i/4)*74);
    }
  }
});
```

Gradient layer creation is made by the `cc.LayerGradient.create` method, which requires both the start and end gradient color in an **RGBA (Red, Green, Blue, Alpha)** format.

There are two things you need to notice about the lines that were added:

1.  The gradient layer should be added before tiles, so tiles will be placed in front of the background because you can play with the depth of the layers to dynamically adjust layers in Z-order, but that's not the case.

2.  Gradient colors can be specified both in decimal (from 0 to 255) and hexadecimal (from 0 x 00 to 0 x FF) values.

Now, test the game again and you should see a nice black to blue background.

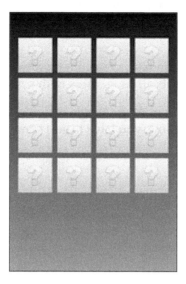

At this time, you have 16 tiles placed on a beautiful gradient background. Now, it's time to let the player have the ability to pick some of them up.

Unfortunately, sprites are just images and can't be picked.

# Extending the Sprite class beyond its capabilities

When I say *sometimes*, I mean *most of the time* the default Cocos2d-JS classes do not let you do everything you need to do with them.

Although this might seem like a limit of Cocos2d-JS, it's one of its best features. You are provided with a basic set of classes you can extend the way you need to, meaning you can add new capabilities.

So, what does it really mean to extend a class? Imagine a real-world example: you're entering a bike shop and buying a mountain bike. Your mountain bike is a class; with this class, you can do everything you can actually do with a mountain bike, namely pedal and steer.

Unfortunately, you are a bit lazy and don't want to pedal all the time, so you buy a little motor and add it to your mountain bike. Now, you can still do everything you usually did with your bike, but you can also rest your legs, turn on the motor, and let it pedal on your behalf.

You just extended the mountain bike, created a motorized mountain bike, which is basically still a bike and inherits all its features with some new ones.

To extend the `Sprite` class and make it capable of doing all the stuff you need in order to make your Concentration game, you have to add some lines to `gamescript.js`:

```
var gameScene = cc.Scene.extend({
  onEnter:function () {
    // same as before
  }
});

var game = cc.Layer.extend({
  init:function () {
    this._super();
    var gradient = cc.LayerGradient.create(cc.c4b(0,0,0,255),
cc.c4b(0x46,0x82,0xB4,255));
    this.addChild(gradient);
    for(i=0;i<16;i++){
      var tile = new MemoryTile();
      this.addChild(tile,0);
      tile.setPosition(49+i%4*74,400-Math.floor(i/4)*74);
    }
  }
});
var MemoryTile = cc.Sprite.extend({
  ctor:function() {
    this._super();
    this.initWithFile("assets/cover.png");
  }
});
```

If you test the game at this time, you will see the same background gradient with the 4 x 4 grid of covered tiles. Let's see what has changed.

Firstly, the tile creation is not made anymore with the following code:

```
var tile = cc.Sprite.create("assets/cover.png");
```

Instead, it's been replaced with:

```
var tile = new MemoryTile();
```

Now, you aren't creating the Sprite itself, but a new type called `MemoryTile`, which will extend the `Sprite` class.

This is how you declare that you are extending a class:

```
var MemoryTile = cc.Sprite.extend({
  ctor:function() {
    this._super();
    this.initWithFile("assets/cover.png");
  }
})
```

Here, the `MemoryTile` variable is declared as an extension of the `Sprite` class.

The `ctor` method is the constructor, basically the stuff being executed as soon as the variable is created. In this case, `initWithFile` assigns the same cover image you assigned before with the old way of placing tiles.

You might argue that four lines of code are being used to do what could be done with just a single line of code, and that's true, but this is the little price you pay to add new functionalities to Cocos2d-JS built-in classes.

Now, you have a new class that extends Sprite. Let's add interactivity to it.

# Making assets react to clicks and touches

There are two ways to pick a tile, irrespective of whether you are playing with a touch or mouse-driven device. You can tap on a tile or you can click on it.

## Picking a tile as an initial attempt

No matter the way you use Cocos2d-JS, all in all you are creating cross-platform games. You have to tell Cocos2d-JS you are going to let the user touch or click on some tiles, so the `MemoryTile` class will change this way:

```
var MemoryTile  = cc.Sprite.extend({
  ctor:function() {
    this._super();
    this.initWithFile("assets/cover.png");
    cc.eventManager.addListener(listener.clone(), this);
  }
})
```

What just happened? You just added an event listener to the event manager. The event manager is the entity that triggers events fired by the game or by the player. The addListener method adds a listener to the event manager, but you don't have a listener at the moment. Let's create one:

```
var listener = cc.EventListener.create({
  event: cc.EventListener.TOUCH_ONE_BY_ONE,
  swallowTouches: true,
  onTouchBegan: function (touch, event) {
    var target = event.getCurrentTarget();
    var location = target.convertToNodeSpace(touch.getLocation());
    var targetSize = target.getContentSize();
    var targetRectangle = cc.rect(0, 0, targetSize.width, targetSize.
height);
    if (cc.rectContainsPoint(targetRectangle, location)) {
      console.log("I picked a tile!!");
    }
  }
})
```

This is the basic listener. You will find yourself using it in most of your projects, so let's take a closer look at it:

```
var listener = cc.EventListener.create({
```

This is how you create a listener with a cc.EventListener.create method. You named it listener to match the previous call:

**cc.eventManager.addListener(listener.clone(), this);**

Then, you modified the MemoryTile class:

```
event: cc.EventListener.TOUCH_ONE_BY_ONE,
```

Here, you specify the type of event: cc.EventListener.TOUCH_ONE_BY_ONE tells the game that you are waiting for touches, but only one at a time. Note that the game talks about touches, but the game will also work with a mouse. This is the true power Cocos2d-JS brings when dealing with cross-platform development.

```
swallowTouches: true,
```

This will basically ignore all touches when there's one active touch:

```
onTouchBegan: function (touch, event) {
```

Now, things start to get serious as you are ready to trigger when the touch or mouse click begins:

```
var target = event.getCurrentTarget();
```

The `getCurrentTarget` method returns the current click target:

```
var location = target.convertToNodeSpace(touch.getLocation());
```

By calling the `touch.getLocation` method, you will have the coordinates of the touch or click inside the game, while the `convertToNodeSpace` method will convert such coordinates into the coordinates relative to the tile itself. This way, the `location` variable will contain the coordinates of the touch or click that is relative to the tile:

```
var targetSize = target.getContentSize();
```

The `getContentSize` function only returns the width and height of the target, in this case the tile:

```
var targetRectangle = cc.rect(0, 0, targetSize.width, targetSize.
height);
```

Now, you define a rectangle with the same size of the tile with the `cc.rect` method. This will allow us to know whether the click or touch action was inside this rectangle. A certain tile has been clicked:

```
if (cc.rectContainsPoint(targetRectangle, location)) {
```

Also, this is how you determine whether a point is inside a rectangle, so you can say that the tile has been clicked.

So, basically:

1.  Each tile detects a `touch` or `click` action, which can be inside or outside the tile itself.
2.  You get touch/click coordinates relative to the tile.
3.  You see whether these coordinates are inside the tile.
4.  You can say which tile has been clicked, if any.

Are you ready to click tiles? Run the game and click on a tile, and you will see.

**I picked a tile!!**

Yes, it works! Let me just show you this line again:

```
cc.eventManager.addListener(listener.clone(), this);
```

Did you notice the `clone()` method when you first wrote it? You used the `clone` method because an event listener can be added only once. The `addListener` method sets a registration flag on the event listener, and it won't add the event listener again if the flag is already set. In other words, you will be able to check for clicks or touches only on the first tile you assigned the listener to.

Using `clone`, you basically duplicate the listener, so each tile will have its own listener up and running.

# Changing sprite images on the fly

Let's now find out how to change sprite images.

## Showing the tile picture

Once a tile is picked, it has to show its picture. Pictures are just a graphical representation of a tile value, which you initially store in an array called `gameArray` declared at the very beginning of a `gamescript.js` file:

```
var gameArray = [0,0,1,1,2,2,3,3,4,4,5,5,6,6,7,7];
vargameScene = cc.Scene.extend({
  onEnter:function () {
    // same as before
  }
});
```

Then, once you create a new tile, you can assign it a custom attribute called `pictureValue` with the value of the *i-th* element of `gameArray`:

```
var game = cc.Layer.extend({
  init:function () {
    this._super();
    var gradient = cc.LayerGradient.create(cc.color(0,0,0,255),
cc.color(0x46,0x82,0xB4,255));
    this.addChild(gradient);
    for(i=0;i<16;i++){
      var tile = new MemoryTile();
      tile.pictureValue = gameArray[i];
      this.addChild(tile,0);
      tile.setPosition(49+i%4*74,400-Math.floor(i/4)*74);
    }
  }
});
```

Also, once the tile is picked, you can again use the `initWithFile()` method to assign it another image according to its value:

```
var listener = cc.EventListener.create({
  event: cc.EventListener.TOUCH_ONE_BY_ONE,
  swallowTouches: true,
  onTouchBegan: function (touch, event) {
    var target = event.getCurrentTarget();
    var location = target.convertToNodeSpace(touch.getLocation());
    var targetSize = target.getContentSize();
    var targetRectangle = cc.rect(0, 0, targetSize.width, targetSize.
height);
    if (cc.rectContainsPoint(targetRectangle, location)) {
      target.initWithFile("assets/tile_"+target.pictureValue+".png");
    }
  }
}
```

Now, it should be clear why the tile images files were numbered from 0 to 7. This is because they will match the tile values assigned by the `gameArray` elements.

Run the game and start picking tiles; see how they uncover showing their actual picture:

Now, add some game logic that will allow you to pick only two tiles, then remove them from the game if they match, or cover them again.

You need another array called `pickedTiles`:

```
Var gameArray = [0,0,1,1,2,2,3,3,4,4,5,5,6,6,7,7];
var pickedTiles = [];
```

Then, you need to add a couple of lines to our `listener` variable:

```
event: cc.EventListener.TOUCH_ONE_BY_ONE,
swallowTouches: true,
onTouchBegan: function (touch, event) {
  if(pickedTiles.length<2){
    var target = event.getCurrentTarget();
    var location = target.convertToNodeSpace(touch.getLocation());
    var targetSize = target.getContentSize();
    var targetRectangle = cc.rect(0, 0, targetSize.width,
targetSize.height);
    if (cc.rectContainsPoint(targetRectangle, location)) {
      if(pickedTiles.indexOf(target)==-1){
        target.initWithFile("assets/tile_"+target.pictureValue+".
png";
        pickedTiles.push(target);
        if(pickedTiles.length==2){
          checkTiles();
        }
      }
    }
  }
})
```

Once the `pickedTiles` array contains two tiles, which prevents the player from picking the same tile twice, then the `checkTiles` function is called.

 I am not explaining much of the code at this step because there's nothing related to Cocos2d-JS; it's just good old JavaScript logic.

```
function checkTiles(){
var listener = cc.EventListener.create({
  function checkTiles(){
    var pause = setTimeout(function(){
      if(pickedTiles[0].pictureValue!=pickedTiles[1].pictureValue){
```

```
            pickedTiles[0].initWithFile("assets/cover.png");
            pickedTiles[1].initWithFile("assets/cover.png");
        }
        else{
          gameLayer.removeChild(pickedTiles[0]);
          gameLayer.removeChild(pickedTiles[1]);
        }
        pickedTiles = [];
    },2000);
}
```

Basically, `checkTiles` waits two seconds, giving some time to the player to memorize the picked tiles, and then again covers tiles if they do not match by simply changing their image to a covered tile again, or removes them from the game with the `removeChild` method.

In both cases, the player will be allowed to pick new tiles by emptying a `pickedTiles` array.

Test the game and make some matches to see the tiles being removed from the game.

Congratulations! You created your first Cocos2d-JS working game. Now, let's add some finishing touches.

# Shuffling the tiles and adding the score

You should have noticed the game isn't that hard, since you are just matching tiles that are one next to each other. The first tile matches the second tile, the third tile matches the fourth, and so on.

First, you need to shuffle the tiles, then you will add the score to the game. Players love to compete for high scores.

You start by adding two new variables scoreText and moves, which will handle the text showing the score and count the number of moves (picks) the player did:

```
Var gameArray = [0,0,1,1,2,2,3,3,4,4,5,5,6,6,7,7];
var pickedTiles = [];
var scoreText;
var moves=0;
```

Then, you need to shuffle gameArray. Shuffling arrays with a true randomization is beyond the scope of this book, so for this game, you are going to use a basic shuffle function you can find at http://jsfromhell.com/array/shuffle:

```
var shuffle = function(v){
for(var j, x, i = v.length; i; j = parseInt(Math.random() * i),
 x = v[--i], v[i] = v[j], v[j] = x);
return v;
};
```

Then gameArray is shuffled at the beginning of the game:

```
vargameScene = cc.Scene.extend({
  onEnter:function () {
    gameArray = shuffle(gameArray);
    this._super();
    gameLayer = new game();
    gameLayer.init();
    this.addChild(gameLayer);
  }
});
```

To add the score text to the game, you need a label. Here is how you can create a text label called `scoreText`, which contains the text `Moves: 0` with a 32 pixel Arial font:

```
var game = cc.Layer.extend({
  init:function () {
    this._super();
    var gradient = cc.LayerGradient.create(cc.color(0,0,0,255),
cc.color(0x46,0x82,0xB4,255));
    this.addChild(gradient);
    scoreText = cc.LabelTTF.create("Moves: 0","Arial","32",cc.TEXT_
ALIGNMENT_CENTER);
    this.addChild(scoreText);
    scoreText.setPosition(90,50);
    for(i=0;i<16;i++){
      var tile = new MemoryTile();
      tile.pictureValue = gameArray[i];
      this.addChild(tile,0);
      tile.setPosition(49+i%4*74,400-Math.floor(i/4)*74);
    }
  }
});
```

Finally, once you check for tile matches, it's easy to increase the number of moves and update the `scoreText` text label with a `setString` method:

```
function checkTiles(){
  moves++;
  scoreText.setString("Moves: "+moves);
  var pause = setTimeout(function(){
    if(pickedTiles[0].pictureValue!=pickedTiles[1].pictureValue){
      pickedTiles[0].initWithFile("assets/cover.png");
      pickedTiles[1].initWithFile("assets/cover.png");
    }
    else{
      gameLayer.removeChild(pickedTiles[0]);
      gameLayer.removeChild(pickedTiles[1]);
    }
    pickedTiles = [];
  },2000);
}
```

Test the script and you will be able to play a full game with a randomly generated board and the score text.

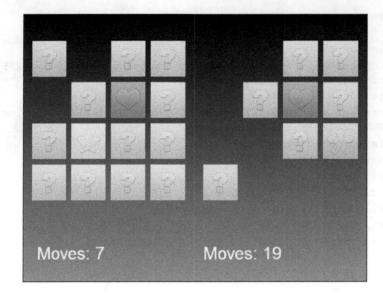

Now, you really do have a complete and polished game!

# Summary

By extending the Sprite class and adding a bit of interactivity, you created your own Concentration game. Now, you also know how to change Sprite images on the fly and deal with text labels.

Concentration is a great brain game. However, sometimes you want more action. To make it harder, you can try making your own 6 x 6 game rather than this easy 4 x 4 game. Head on to the next chapter and let's make things move!

# 3
# Moving Sprites Around the Screen – An Endless Runner

A while ago, endless runners started with a game called **Helicopter** where you had to drive a helicopter through an endless cave, just pressing a button to give it thrust.

Then, games became more complex until mobile gaming started to spread. Endless runners started gaining a new popularity due to their simple one tap control. The player is just required to touch anywhere when needed to control a helicopter.

In this chapter, you are going to build an endless runner that features a spaceship flying through a city while avoiding dangerous asteroids.

In the making of this game, you will learn, among other things, how to:

- Scroll big images to give an idea on an endless background
- Schedule events
- Control a frame rate
- Check collision between sprites
- Create a simple particle system
- Move sprites manually or using actions

Moreover, although this is supposed to be a cross-platform game, you will also learn about mouse-only controls. It will be easy to change them to touch or tap controls as you already met them during the making of Concentration. All in all, it's something you can find useful should you plan a desktop-only browser game.

# Loading and placing graphic resources

You need to build the game over the blueprint created in the first chapter, so here is the content of the `assets` folder:

You can see the spaceship, the asteroid you have to avoid, a small circle to create particle effects, and the scrolling background.

You will spend some time trying to understand the background. As the game is 480 x 320 pixels, your background should be at least *480\*2=960* pixels wide, which is made by two 480 x 320 seamless images.

With the following image, you will be able to give the player the possibility to fly through an endless cityscape:

All these images need to be preloaded by the `loadassets.js` file located in `src`, which will become:

```
var gameResources = ["assets/background.png","assets/ship.png",
"assets/particle.png","assets/asteroid.png"
];
```

You also need to make some changes to `main.js` because this time you want a game in the landscape mode:

```
cc.game.onStart = function(){
  cc.view.setDesignResolutionSize(480, 320, cc.ResolutionPolicy.SHOW_
ALL);
  cc.LoaderScene.preload(gameResources, function () {
    cc.director.runScene(new gameScene());
  }, this);
};
cc.game.run();
```

The highlighted line shows the new resolution settings.

# Adding an endless scrolling background

Now, it's time to add the cityscape background, which will scroll endlessly and seamlessly. Finally, you can start editing `gamescript.js`:

```
var background;
var gameLayer;
var scrollSpeed = 1;
var gameScene = cc.Scene.extend({
  onEnter:function () {
    this._super();
    gameLayer = new game();
    gameLayer.init();
    this.addChild(gameLayer);
  }
});
var game = cc.Layer.extend({
  init:function () {
    this._super();
    background = new ScrollingBG();
    this.addChild(background);
```

```
        this.scheduleUpdate();
      },
    update:function(dt){
      background.scroll();
    }
  });
  var ScrollingBG = cc.Sprite.extend({
    ctor:function() {
      this._super();
      this.initWithFile("assets/background.png");
    },
    onEnter:function() {
      this.setPosition(480,160);
    },
    scroll:function(){
      this.setPosition(this.getPosition().
        x-scrollSpeed,this.getPosition().y);
      if(this.getPosition().x<0){
        this.setPosition(this.getPosition().x+480,this.getPosition().y);
      }
    }
  });
```

You might think that's a lot of code, but most of it is just a copy and paste of what you've already seen in the making of the Concentration game.

Let's have a look at the interesting new stuff:

```
var background;
var gameLayer;
var scrollSpeed = 1;
```

These three variables will represent the background sprite, the main game layer, and the scrolling speed in pixels per frame. This means you want the background to scroll by one pixel at each frame, that is, 60 pixels per second.

Now, it should be really clear why you are working with a fixed frame rate. On fast bowsers such as Chrome with a 120 fps refresh, you will able to see the background scrolling at the same speed as on the Firefox 60 fps browser.

The `gameScene` code does not contain anything new, so let's jump to game definition, which will introduce a new feature:

```
var game = cc.Layer.extend({
  init:function () {
    this._super();
    background = new ScrollingBG();
    this.addChild(background);
    this.scheduleUpdate();
  },
  update:function(dt){
    background.scroll();
  }
});
```

After declaring a `ScrollingBG` class, you will extend the built-in `Sprite` class in the same way you did in the making of Concentration when you created the tiles; you can see a call to `scheduleUpdate` method.

Normally, a Cocos2d-JS game is static. It never updates. Like the previous Concentration game, if you leave the game alone for ages, nothing happens.

To help you add some actions, Cocos2d-JS allows you to schedule events that happen at a certain time.

The easiest way to schedule an event is the `scheduleUpdate` method. It's just like saying you want to do something each time the game is refreshed, which in our case is every 1/60 seconds.

When you call `scheduleUpdate`, a custom `update` function will be called at each frame:

```
update:function(dt){
background.scroll();
}
```

At the moment, you are just calling a custom method of your `ScrollingBG` new class.

The definition of `ScrollingBG` is also quite simple if you got the basics of class inheritance explained in the previous chapter:

```
var ScrollingBG = cc.Sprite.extend({
  ctor:function() {
    this._super();
    this.initWithFile("assets/background.png");
  },
  onEnter:function() {
    this.setPosition(480,160);
  },
  scroll:function(){
    this.setPosition(this.getPosition().x-scrollSpeed,this.
getPosition().y);
    if(this.getPosition().x<0){
      this.setPosition(this.getPosition().x+480,this.getPosition().y);
    }
  }
});
```

Here, once you load and add the background image to the screen, you move it by the `scrollSpeed` pixels to the left, giving the feeling that it is moving to the right. Once you moved the background image by more than 480 pixels, that is, half of its length or the full length of your game resolution, you move it back by exactly 480 pixels to give the player the illusion of an infinite scrolling.

I could place a picture of what you get at this point, but it's much better if you test it yourself and see a beautiful scrolling background.

Note this is just one way to move assets around the screen as Cocos2d-JS offers a set of methods to manage sprite positions. I will cover them when adding asteroids on the screen, but at the moment, let's focus on the main actor of the game: the spaceship!

# Adding the spaceship

The spaceship you are going to add is just another sprite, but you are going to give it behavior like it was ruled by gravity.

First, let' s add a couple of variables:

```
var background;
var gameLayer;
var scrollSpeed = 1;
var ship;
var gameGravity = -0.05;
```

The `ship` variable will be the spaceship itself, whereas `gameGravity` is the force that will attract the spaceship toward the bottom of the screen.

Then, inside the `init` function in `game` declaration, you add the ship in the same way you added the background:

```
var game = cc.Layer.extend({
  init:function () {
    this._super();
    background = new ScrollingBG();
    this.addChild(background);
    this.scheduleUpdate();
    ship = new Ship();
    this.addChild(ship);
  },
  update:function(dt){
    background.scroll();
    ship.updateY();
  }
});
```

Then, in the `update` function (remember this function is automatically called at each frame). Thanks to the `scheduleUpdate` method, an `updateY` custom method is called.

The creation of the ship itself does not differ much from just extending the `Sprite` class:

```
var Ship = cc.Sprite.extend({
  ctor:function() {
    this._super();
    this.initWithFile("assets/ship.png");
    this.ySpeed = 0;
  },
  onEnter:function() {
    this.setPosition(60,160);
  },
  updateY:function() {
    this.setPosition(this.getPosition().x,this.getPosition().y+this.
ySpeed);
    this.ySpeed += gameGravity;
  }
});
```

The spaceship is assigned an image and a custom attribute called ySpeed, initially set to zero from the ctor constructor.

Once it's placed on the stage, the onEnter function places it at 60, 160 (remember its *x* position will never change). Then, the setPosition function, which is called at each frame by the game's update function adds gameGravity value to the ship's vertical speed (ySpeed) and updates its *y* position by adding speed to the current position.

This is the cheapest but quickest way to handle gravity, forces, and thrust (that will be introduced in the next step), and it works well in simple games like an endless runner.

Now, run the game and see what happens:

You should see our previously created nice scrolling background and our poor spaceship falling down and disappearing off the bottom of the screen.

You just learned the first rule of spaceship creation: *remember the engine*.

# Controlling the spaceship

Players will be able to give thrust to the spaceship by holding the mouse or finger pressed on the screen.

As you should be able to detect when the player touches the screen, I am going to show you a mouse-only way to control the spaceship to make you learn something new. You are free to replace this way to control the ship with the one you prefer.

You are going to manage ship control in just a few lines, first by adding a new global variable:

```
var background;
var gameLayer;
var scrollSpeed = 1;
var ship;
var gameGravity = -0.05;
var gameThrust = 0.1;
```

The `gameThrust` variable represents engine power, the force that will make the ship fly through the air.

You are controlling the game with the mouse, so that's how you change the `game` declaration:

```
var game = cc.Layer.extend({
  init:function () {
    this._super();
    cc.eventManager.addListener({
      event: cc.EventListener.MOUSE,
      onMouseDown: function(event){
        ship.engineOn = true;
      },
      onMouseUp: function(event){
        ship.engineOn = false;
      }
    },this)
    background = new ScrollingBG();
    this.addChild(background);
    this.scheduleUpdate();
    ship = new Ship();
    this.addChild(ship);

  },
  update:function(dt){
    background.scroll();
    ship.updateY();
  }
});
```

Unlike in the previous chapter, here you added the listener on the fly without declaring it as a variable and then calling it. It's basically the same as before, it's just that now you are working with the mouse, so you must define the event type as `cc.EventListener.MOUSE`. The events are `onMouseDown` when the player presses the mouse and `onMouseUp` when the mouse is released. Now, with `onMouseDown` and `onMouseUp`, you just turn the ship's engine to on or off, which is actually a Boolean `ship` attribute called `engineOn`.

What are you going to do with such an attribute? You just update the ship's vertical speed just like you did with the gravity:

```
var Ship = cc.Sprite.extend({
  ctor:function() {
    this._super();
    this.initWithFile("assets/ship.png");
    this.ySpeed = 0;
    this.engineOn = false;
  },
  onEnter:function() {
    this.setPosition(60,160);
  },
  updateY:function() {
    if(this.engineOn){
      this.ySpeed += gameThrust;
    }
    this.setPosition(this.getPosition().x,this.getPosition().y+this.
ySpeed);
    this.ySpeed += gameGravity;
  }
})
```

This was really easy. First, you set `engineOn` to `false` and according to its value, you decide whether you have to add `gameThrust` to `ySpeed`.

Test the game and try to control the ship by pressing and releasing the mouse button.

Finally, the spaceship can fly through the city in peace and harmony. Unfortunately, game designers are a bit mad and they could decide to make some changes to spaceship plans by adding a belt of deadly asteroids big enough to smash a spaceship.

# Adding asteroids

As the spaceship flies from left to right (actually it does not, but that's how it seems), you have to add asteroids, which enter the screen from the right-hand side of the game.

Now, you can just place some asteroid sprites on the right-hand side of the screen and make them move to the left-hand side just like you did with the background cityscape, but you wouldn't learn anything new if you did that, so let's see another way to manage sprite movement.

First things first, before you can move an asteroid, you have to create it.

In this game, a new asteroid will appear every half a second, so it's time to schedule another event in the game class declaration:

```
var game = cc.Layer.extend({
  init:function () {
    this._super();
    cc.eventManager.addListener({
      event: cc.EventListener.MOUSE,
      onMouseDown: function(event){
        ship.engineOn = true;
      },
      onMouseUp: function(event){
        ship.engineOn = false;
      }
    },this)
    background = new ScrollingBG();
    this.addChild(background);
    this.scheduleUpdate();
    this.schedule(this.addAsteroid,0.5);
    ship = new Ship();
    this.addChild(ship);

  },
  update:function(dt){
    background.scroll();
```

```
        ship.updateY();
    },
    addAsteroid:function(event){
        var asteroid = new Asteroid();
        this.addChild(asteroid,1);
    },
    removeAsteroid:function(asteroid){
        this.removeChild(asteroid);
    }
});
```

To schedule an event at a given interval, you use the schedule method that works
like scheduleUpdate, but this time you can also define which function to call,
addAsteroid, in this case, and the interval of time in seconds.

It's easy to see what addAsteroid does: it adds an asteroid by extending the Sprite
class in the same way you saw before. You also added a removeAsteroid function
because you don't want asteroids to remain in the game forever; you will see how to
remove them once they are not necessary anymore.

This is the Asteroid class:

```
var Asteroid = cc.Sprite.extend({
    ctor:function() {
        this._super();
        this.initWithFile("assets/asteroid.png");
    },
    onEnter:function() {
        this._super();
        this.setPosition(600,Math.random()*320);
        var moveAction= cc.MoveTo.create(2.5, new cc.Point(-100,Math.
random()*320));
        this.runAction(moveAction);
        this.scheduleUpdate();
    },
    update:function(dt){
        if(this.getPosition().x<-50){
            gameLayer.removeAsteroid(this)
        }
    }
});
```

Run the game and you will see an asteroid belt flying towards the ship following a random path.

There is a lot of stuff in a simple class declaration, so let's take a closer look at the preceding code.

The `ctor` constructor simply creates the instance and assigns it an image, as usual. So, the magic happened somewhere else.

The `onEnter` event places the asteroid on the right-hand side of the screen at a random height; the next line is responsible for the whole animation:

```
var moveAction = cc.MoveTo.create(2.5,
  new cc.Point(-100,Math.random()*320));
```

Cocos2d-JS allows you to create actions, which in this case basically are tweens and can be seen as things to do at a given point in time.

This action should move to a given random point on the left-hand side of the screen in 2.5 seconds. That's it. It doesn't matter how Cocos2d-JS will perform this task; you just say *bring this asteroid and make it fly to that point*.

The power of these actions is awesome and you will deal with it in more examples in this book.

Once the action is created, you make Cocos2d-JS execute it with:

```
this.runAction(moveAction);
```

The asteroid travel is done. You should also see whether there's a `scheduleUpdate` call because you want to remove asteroids once they exit from the left-hand side of the screen; so, in the `update` function (remember, every `scheduleUpdate` method calls an `update` function at each frame). You simply check when the asteroid is outside the screen and eventually remove it with the `removeAsteroid` method you created before.

That was really easy, wasn't it?

Too bad! The asteroids and spaceship do not collide yet, but don't worry, it won't take more than a couple of lines.

# Asteroid versus spaceship collision

The easiest way to see whether two sprites collide, which is also the most used in simple fast paced arcade games like the one you are currently building, is by checking whether sprite bounding boxes intersect somehow.

The bounding box of an image is the smallest rectangle, which entirely contains the image itself, and the principle of this method can be explained by the following image:

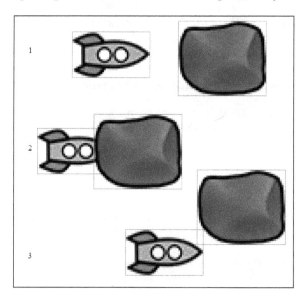

In this 4x zoomed image, you can see the three different ways the bounding box collision will react:

1. Bounding boxes do not intersect. There is no collision.
2. Bounding boxes intersect. There is a collision.
3. Bounding boxes intersect, although there isn't a collision.

In sophisticated collision engines, to prevent case 3, once bounding boxes intersect, a pixel perfect collision is performed, but this is CPU-consuming and at the moment, you don't want such a high level of precision.

So, if you want to make case 3 occur as seldom as possible, you can draw your sprites with shapes as close to a rectangle as possible, or you can consider the intersection between two boxes a little smaller than the original bounding boxes.

Remember, players want to be forgiven, so if it's just a matter of a couple of pixels, it's better not to see an actual collision rather than to see a false positive collision.

Having said that, here is how Cocos2d-JS will help you to manage bounding box collisions working on asteroid's `update` function:

```
update:function(dt){
    var shipBoundingBox = ship.getBoundingBox();
    var asteroidBoundingBox = this.getBoundingBox();
    if(cc.rectIntersectsRect(shipBoundingBox,asteroidBoundingBox)){
        gameLayer.removeAsteroid(this);
        restartGame();
    }
    if(this.getPosition().x<-50){
        gameLayer.removeAsteroid(this)
    }
}
```

The `getBoundingBox` method returns a rectangle, which is the actual sprite bounding box, and the `rectIntersectsRect` method checks whether two rectangles intersect.

This is easy. Collision detection occurs in two lines. Then, the asteroid is removed and the `restartGame` function is called. This function just resets spaceship's variables, as shown in the following code:

```
function restartGame(){
    ship.ySpeed = 0;
    ship.setPosition(ship.getPosition().x,160);
}
```

Now, test the game and you will see the spaceship position being reset once it collides with an asteroid. This way, the game becomes a bit punishing when you die, as you will often respawn in front of an asteroid, causing an immediate death. Remember, players want to be forgiven.

# Invulnerability

This feature has nothing to do with the new Cocos2d-JS stuff, it's just some polishing in game design, but remember polishing is always better than adding features.

People played Angry Birds series to death because it's polished, not because wooden blocks did break exactly like a real-world wooden block would.

So, after the player smashed the spaceship into an asteroid, let's make the spaceship invulnerable for a limited period of time; let the player see the ship cannot be destroyed by making it flash.

You are going to add an `invulnerability` attribute to the spaceship in the ship's `ctor` constructor:

```
ctor:function() {
    this._super();
    this.initWithFile("assets/ship.png");
    this.ySpeed = 0;
this.engineOn = false;
this.invulnerability = 0;
}
```

When `invulnerability` is set to zero, this means the spaceship is not invulnerable and can be destroyed by asteroids. You have to add this case to Asteroid's `update` method:

```
update:function(dt){
    var shipBoundingBox = ship.getBoundingBox();
    var asteroidBoundingBox = this.getBoundingBox();
    if(cc.rectIntersectsRect(shipBoundingBox,asteroidBoundingBox)
&&ship.invulnerability==0){
        gameLayer.removeAsteroid(this);
        restartGame();
    }
    if(this.getPosition().x<-50){
        gameLayer.removeAsteroid(this)
    }
}
```

As you can see, collision is processed only if invulnerability is set to zero, and when you restart the game in the `restartGame` function, you assign it a high value, let's say 100:

```
function restartGame(){
    ship.ySpeed = 0;
    ship.setPosition(ship.getPosition().x,160);
ship.invulnerability=100;
}
```

This means that now the spaceship cannot be destroyed. To give the player a visual feedback and decrease invulnerability, let's add two lines to ship's `updateY` function:

```
updateY:function() {
if(this.engineOn){
    this.ySpeed += gameThrust;
  }
if(this.invulnerability>0){
    this.invulnerability --;
    this.setOpacity(255-this.getOpacity());
  }
this.setPosition(this.getPosition().x,this.getPosition().y+this.
ySpeed);
  this.ySpeed += gameGravity;
}
```

If invulnerability is greater than zero, decrease it and make the spaceship flash by switching its opacity from fully opaque (255) to completely transparent (0).

The `setOpacity` and `getOpacity` methods handle sprite's opacity.

Test the game and after you run into an asteroid, you should have *God mode* enabled for about a second and a half.

# Preventing the spaceship from flying off the screen

The last thing you need to do is prevent the spaceship from flying off the screen. If you press the mouse for too long, or if you don't press the mouse at all, your ship will fly respectively off the top or the bottom of the screen.

You need to prevent the ship from flying off the screen by punishing it with death.

Just add these two lines to the ship's `updateY` function:

```
updateY:function() {
if(this.engineOn){
    this.ySpeed += gameThrust;
  }
if(this.invulnerability>0){
    this.invulnerability --;
    this.setOpacity(255-this.getOpacity());
  }
```

```
   this.setPosition(this.getPosition().x,this.getPosition().y+this.
ySpeed);
   this.ySpeed += gameGravity;
if(this.getPosition().y<0 || this.getPosition().y>320){
   restartGame();
   }
}
```

No need to comment them, it's just an `if` statement that checks for the spaceship's vertical position.

# Adding particles

Do you remember that in your `assets` folder, there's a yellow circle called `particle.png`? You will use it to create a nice particle effect to simulate the spaceship engine.

Discussing particle systems is beyond the scope of this book, so for more detailed information as well as complete particle generation software compatible with Cocos2d-JS, take a look at `https://71squared.com/particledesigner`.

Here, you are just going to add the simplest particle effect ever, but you will see it has a visual appeal like the following figure:

First, create a new global variable:

```
var background;
var gameLayer;
var scrollSpeed = 1;
var ship;
var gameGravity = -0.05;
var gameThrust = 0.1;
var emitter;
```

The emitter will be created and configured in game's `init` function:

```
init:function () {
  this._super();
  this.setMouseEnabled(true);
  background = new ScrollingBG();
  this.addChild(background);
  this.scheduleUpdate();
  this.schedule(this.addAsteroid,0.5)
  ship = new Ship();
  this.addChild(ship);
  emitter = cc.ParticleSun.create();
  this.addChild(emitter,1);
  var myTexture = cc.textureCache. addImage("assets/particle.png");
  emitter.setTexture(myTexture);
  emitter.setStartSize(2);
  emitter.setEndSize(4);
}
```

Here, you can see that the emitter is created with a **sun** effect, an image is assigned to it, and a start and end image size are given to it.

This is enough to generate an ever working particle emitter, but you also need it to follow the spaceship only when the engines are working by updating the ship's `updateY` function:

```
updateY:function() {
  if(this.engineOn){
    this.ySpeed += gameThrust;
    emitter.setPosition(this.getPosition().x-25,
this.getPosition().y);
  }
  else{
    emitter.setPosition(this.getPosition().x-250,
this.getPosition().y);
```

```
    }
    if(this.invulnerability>0){
        this.invulnerability --;
        this.setOpacity(255-this.getOpacity());
    }
this.setPosition(this.getPosition().x,this.getPosition().y+this.
ySpeed);
    this.ySpeed += gameGravity;
    if(this.getPosition().y<0 || this.getPosition().y>320){
        restartGame();
    }

}
```

Here, you just move the emitter to spaceship's tail when the engine is on, and outside the screen when the engine is off. Cheap and dirty, but it's working.

Test the game; you should see an eye-candy effect when engines are on, just like in the image you saw before.

# Summary

In this chapter, you learned how to create tweens, collisions, and so on. You also learned how to pass through particle generation and create a complete working game.

There is something you should do to get more familiar with Cocos2d-JS, that is, use what you learned until now and improve the game. You can try to switch the control mode from mouse-driven to touch-driven, display text with the maximum distance travelled without hitting an asteroid, and increase the difficulty level every $n$ seconds without hitting asteroids by making asteroids faster or appear more often.

Now, you are ready to dive into the next chapter where touch controls will become more interactive thanks to swipe detection.

# Learn about Swipes through the making of Sokoban

Do you know the Sokoban game? It's a funny puzzle game featuring a player pushing crates to some designated places. Normally, on a computer, these kinds of games — called tile-based games — are controlled by arrow keys, but since our game has to be cross-platform, we will let the player control in-game movements using swipes.

The game we will build is very similar to an iOS game I made called BWBan. It's free; you can play it at `http://bit.ly/1fUXP8c`.

In the process of making this game, which we'll call Cocosban, you will learn about the following topics:

- How to detect swipes
- How to load graphic assets through a sprite sheet
- How to create 8-bit-like pixel games by playing with anti-aliasing

There's a lot to do, so let's start with the good old blueprint made in the first chapter and work on it.

# Loading graphic assets

Needless to say, the first thing you should do is place your graphic assets in the assets folder, but there is something new about this step.

In previous examples, we always filled our assets folder with one PNG image for each game actor — the spaceship and asteroid had their own image. This also applies for all Concentration tiles and so on.

Cocos2d-JS has no problems in dealing with multiple images, but as a golden rule, remember the less images you have to deal with, the better your game performs.

So, where's the trick? In order to have a spaceship and an asteroid, you would think you have to load a spaceship image and an asteroid image, but there's another better way to do it, using **sprite sheets**.

A sprite sheet is a single image made by combining various small images into it. If you are in to web designing, they are called **CSS sprites**, and if you have already made some native iOS applications, they are called texture atlases.

Does this mean that you have to manually create a large image and place all your graphic assets inside of it? Well, although you can do it manually, there are several software solutions to speed up the process. The one I use and recommend to you is TexturePacker, which you can find at www.codeandweb.com/texturepacker. It works with an intuitive drag-and-drop interface and supports Cocos2d export.

These are the four images I created for the game, directly from my Photoshop:

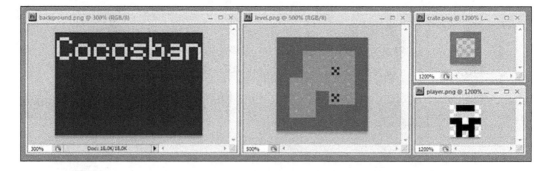

I would like you to notice the zoom factor of the images — actually, they are really tiny. Since we are making a pixel game, the image I made are really small, from 96 x 64 pixels for the title image down to 5 x 5 pixels for the crate and the player.

Once processed by TexturePacker and exported to Cocos2d, your assets folder should contain the following two files:

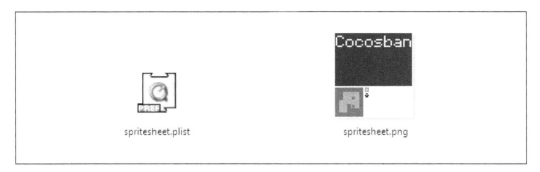

You should easily recognize all previously drawn graphic assets packed into spritesheet.png, and you will wonder why we need the spritesheet.plist file.

Open it and you will basically find an XML file with all the information for the images, from their original file names to their current sizes and coordinates inside spritesheet.plist:

```
<?xml version="1.0" encoding="UTF-8"?>
<!DOCTYPEplist PUBLIC "-//Apple Computer//DTD PLIST 1.0//EN" "http://
www.apple.com/DTDs/PropertyList-1.0.dtd">
<plist version="1.0">
    <dict>
        <key>frames</key>
        <dict>
            <key>background.png</key>
            <dict>
                <key>frame</key>
                <string>{{2,2},{96,64}}</string>
                <key>offset</key>
                <string>{0,0}</string>
                <key>rotated</key>
                <false/>
                <key>sourceColorRect</key>
                <string>{{0,0},{96,64}}</string>
                <key>sourceSize</key>
                <string>{96,64}</string>
            </dict>
            <key>crate.png</key>
            <dict>
                <key>frame</key>
```

```
            <string>{{39,68},{5,5}}</string>
            <key>offset</key>
            <string>{0,0}</string>
            <key>rotated</key>
            <false/>
            <key>sourceColorRect</key>
            <string>{{0,0},{5,5}}</string>
            <key>sourceSize</key>
            <string>{5,5}</string>
          </dict>
        </dict>
      </plist>
```

In various Cocos2d-JS guides and references, this is referred to as a sprite sheet. Actually, it's more of a texture atlas; thanks to the XML file, which explains and describes each image included in the sheet.

So, it's time to load both files with `loadassets.js`:

```
var gameResources = [
  "assets/spritesheet.plist",
  "assets/spritesheet.png"
];
```

Meanwhile, `main.js` will set our resolution policy at 480 x 320 pixels in portrait mode:

```
cc.game.onStart = function(){
  cc.view.setDesignResolutionSize(480, 320, cc.ResolutionPolicy.SHOW_
ALL);
  cc.LoaderScene.preload(gameResources, function () {
    cc.director.runScene(new gameScene());
  }, this);
};
cc.game.run();

varmyGame = new cocos2dGame(gameScene);
```

Now, it's time to create the game itself.

# Building a level

Normally, tile-based levels are stored in two-dimensional arrays, and Cocosban follows this trend. So, the first global variable we'll declare in `gamescript.js`, which is an array containing level data, is as follows:

```
var level = [
  [1,1,1,1,1,1,1],
  [1,1,0,0,0,0,1],
  [1,1,3,0,2,0,1],
  [1,0,0,4,0,0,1],
  [1,0,3,1,2,0,1],
  [1,0,0,1,1,1,1],
  [1,1,1,1,1,1,1]
];
```

Each item represents a tile, and each value represents an item, which I coded this way:

- `0`: This item is an empty tile
- `1`: This item is a wall
- `2`: This item is the place where to drop a crate
- `3`: This item is the crate
- `4`: This item is the player
- `5`: This item is the crate on a place where to drop a crate (3+2)
- `6`: This item is the player on a place where to drop a crate (4+2)

Our `gameScene` declaration is always the same:

```
var gameScene = cc.Scene.extend({
  onEnter:function () {
  this._super();
    gameLayer = new game();
    gameLayer.init();
    this.addChild(gameLayer);
  }
});
```

And finally, we are ready to extend the `game` class.

Before we start, I want to quickly discuss mobile tile-based games.

If you look at the `level` array, you will see it's a *7x7=49* items array. This means we are going to place *49 tiles = 49 sprites* on the screen.

That's OK, but placing stuff on the screen costs performance. Since we don't know on which devices our game will run, the less potentially moving stuff on the screen, the better the performances.

Since the only moving stuff in our game are the crates and the hero, while all wall and floor tiles always remain in their place, I simply hand-drew the level, adding only moveable characters as tiles.

You should do the same when designing for cross-platform purposes unless you are using random or procedurally generated content.

That said, this is how the game class is declared:

```
var game   = cc.Layer.extend({
  init:function () {
    this._super();
    cache = cc.spriteFrameCache;
    cache.addSpriteFrames("assets/spritesheet.plist", "assets/
spritesheet.png");
    var backgroundSprite = cc.Sprite.create(cache.
getSpriteFrame("background.png"));
    backgroundSprite.setPosition(240,160);
    backgroundSprite.setScale(5);
    this.addChild(backgroundSprite);
    var levelSprite =  cc.Sprite.create(cache.getSpriteFrame("level.
png"));
    levelSprite.setPosition(240,110);
    levelSprite.setScale(5);
    this.addChild(levelSprite);
  }
```

As you can see, most of the code has already been explained in the previous chapters. We enable the game to be touch-driven and add some sprites on the stage. Just look at how I am loading the sprite sheet:

```
cache = cc.spriteFrameCache;
cache.addSpriteFrames("assets/spritesheet.plist", "assets/spritesheet.
png");
```

And this is how you can select a single image from a sprite sheet:

```
var backgroundSprite = cc.Sprite.create(cache.
getSpriteFrame("background.png"));
```

Finally, since our sprites are very, very tiny, they need to be scaled up. The `setScale` method allows us to scale sprites:

```
backgroundSprite.setScale(5);
```

Now, we are ready to launch the game and see our sprites scaled up by 5x:

The preceding image is not a blurred, low-resolution image. It's the actual game as you will see on the screen, because Cocos2d-JS applies an anti-aliasing effect, which, in this case, wastes the 8-bit look we wanted to give the game. Anti-aliasing is very useful when you want to get smooth images, but will make your game look really bad if you plan to create a pixel game.

You can prevent anti-aliasing from being applied to a texture with the `setAliasTexParameters` method by just adding this line:

```
var game   = cc.Layer.extend({
  init:function () {
    this._super();
    cache = cc.spriteFrameCache;
    cache.addSpriteFrames("assets/spritesheet.plist", "assets/
spritesheet.png");
    var backgroundSprite = cc.Sprite.create(cache.
getSpriteFrame("background.png"));
    backgroundSprite.getTexture().setAliasTexParameters();
```

```
        backgroundSprite.setPosition(240,160);
        backgroundSprite.setScale(5);
        this.addChild(backgroundSprite);
        var levelSprite =  cc.Sprite.create(cache.getSpriteFrame("level.
png"));
        levelSprite.setPosition(240,110);
        levelSprite.setScale(5);
        this.addChild(levelSprite);
    }
});
```

Run the game again, and you will see your pixel-perfect game:

Also, I would like you to notice that the `setAliasTexParameters` method is called once and works on both sprites—and will work on every other sprite created in this game—because it's applied on the whole sprite sheet.

At this time, we can create the player and the crates. They are just sprites manually positioned in the right place according to their position in the `level` array and the position of the level image in the stage.

The rest of the script to build the level has nothing to do with Cocos2d-JS since it's pure JavaScript, so I am going to speed up a bit. First, I need three more global variables:

```
var cratesArray = [];
var playerPosition;
var playerSprite;
```

This is what they represent:

- `cratesArray`: This is the array that will contain all crate sprites
- `playerPosition`: This is the variable that will be used to store a player's position inside the maze
- `playerSprite`: This variable represents the player itself

Then, after the line that added the `level` sprite, we can place the player and the crates:

```
var game  = cc.Layer.extend({
  init:function () {
    this._super();
    // same as before
    this.addChild(levelSprite);
    for(i=0;i<7;i++){
      cratesArray[i]=[];
      for(j=0;j<7;j++){
        switch(level[i][j]){
          case 4:
          case 6:
          playerSprite = cc.Sprite.create(cache.
getSpriteFrame("player.png"));
          playerSprite.setPosition(165+25*j,185-25*i);
          playerSprite.setScale(5);
          this.addChild(playerSprite);
          playerPosition = {x:j,y:i};
          cratesArray[i][j]=null;
          break;
          case 3:
          case 5:
          var crateSprite = cc.Sprite.create(cache.
getSpriteFrame("crate.png"));
          crateSprite.setPosition(165+25*j,185-25*i);
          crateSprite.setScale(5);
          this.addChild(crateSprite);
          cratesArray[i][j]=crateSprite;
          break;
          default:
          cratesArray[i][j]=null;
        }
      }
    }
  }
});
```

Did you see? Through pure JavaScript, we just added the crate sprite when the `level` array item is 3 or 5 and the player sprite when the `level` array item is 4 or 6.

The strange math operations are just used to place tiles in the right place according to their position.

This following screenshot is the result you should see when you run the script:

And that's it! You have your pixel level ready to be played. Let's detect player movements.

# Detecting swipes

If we analyze a swipe, we can break it down into three parts:

1. The player is touching the stage at a certain point.
2. The player is dragging their finger in a certain direction.
3. The player is releasing the finger.

By comparing the coordinates of the points where the drag started and ended, we can determine the direction of the swipe and move the player accordingly.

We need to add three new global variables:

```
var startTouch;
var endTouch;
var swipeTolerance = 10;
```

Their names are quite self-explicative: `startTouch` and `endTouch` will store the starting and ending points of the swipe, while `swipeTolerance` is the minimum allowed distance in pixels between `startTouch` and `endTouch` in order to consider the whole action as a swipe.

Now, we will let `game` detect when a touch starts or ends:

```
var game   = cc.Layer.extend({
  init:function () {
    // same as before
    cc.eventManager.addListener(listener, this);
    }
});
```

As usual, we added a listener attached to a variable called `listener`, which we'll define this way:

```
var listener = cc.EventListener.create({
  event: cc.EventListener.TOUCH_ONE_BY_ONE,
  swallowTouches: true,
  onTouchBegan:function (touch,event) {
    startTouch = touch.getLocation();
    return true;
  },
  onTouchEnded:function(touch, event){
    endTouch = touch.getLocation();
    swipeDirection();
  }
});
```

The onTouchBegan function will register the initial touch and update the startTouch content; thanks to the getLocation method. Also, notice the function returns true. It's very important you make this function return true, or onTouchEnded won't be triggered.

The same applies for onTouchEnded, which will update endTouch. Then, the swipeDirection function is called. It will allow us to move the player:

```
function swipeDirection(){
   var distX = startTouch.x - endTouch.x;
   var distY = startTouch.y - endTouch.y;
   if(Math.abs(distX)+Math.abs(distY)>swipeTolerance){
     if(Math.abs(distX)>Math.abs(distY)){
        if(distX>0){
          playerSprite.setPosition(playerSprite.getPosition().
             x-25,playerSprite.getPosition().y);
          //move(-1,0);
        }
        else{
          playerSprite.setPosition(playerSprite.getPosition().
             x+25,playerSprite.getPosition().y);
          //move(1,0);
        }
     }
     else{
        if(distY>0){
          playerSprite.setPosition(playerSprite.getPosition().
             x,playerSprite.getPosition().y-25);
          //move(0,1);
        }
        else{
          playerSprite.setPosition(playerSprite.getPosition().
             x,playerSprite.getPosition().y+25);
          //move(0,-1);
        }
     }
   }
}
```

Run the game and the following screenshot is what you will see:

Once you swipe in a direction, the player moves accordingly.

Let's see what happens in the `swipeDirection` function:

```
var distX = startTouch.x - endTouch.x;
var distY = startTouch.y - endTouch.y;
```

Horizontal and vertical distances from the start to the end of the touch are calculated:

```
if(Math.abs(distX)+Math.abs(distY)>swipeTolerance){
```

The whole function is executed only if the sum of horizontal and vertical distances is greater than the minimum pixel tolerance allowed to say that the movement is actually a swipe:

```
if(Math.abs(distX)>Math.abs(distY)){
```

The next step is to determine whether the player swiped horizontally or vertically. There's no check to see whether a swipe was strictly horizontal or vertical; so, diagonal swipes will be seen as either horizontal or vertical, according to their biggest component:

```
if(distX>0){
```

Once we know whether the movement is horizontal or vertical, it's time to check for the direction: left or right? Up or down? The rest of the code just checks for these questions and moves the player by 25 pixels accordingly. Unfortunately, you will be able to walk through crates and walls. It's time to code game rules.

# Completing the game

The code I am about to write has nothing to do with Cocos2d-JS as it's just plain JavaScript, and explaining it would go beyond the scope of this book. I am just checking for legal moves and will move the player and the crates accordingly.

Everything is managed by the move function, which will check for legal moves and update crates and player positions. The move function has two arguments, deltaX and deltaY, which represent the amount of tiles the player is trying to move horizontally or vertically.

This means move(0,1) will try to move the player up (0 tiles horizontally, 1 tile vertically), move(-1,0) will try to move the player left, and so on.

The swipeDirection function changes this:

```
function swipeDirection(){
  var distX = startTouch.x - endTouch.x;
  var distY = startTouch.y - endTouch.y;
  if(Math.abs(distX)+Math.abs(distY)>swipeTolerance){
    if(Math.abs(distX)>Math.abs(distY)){
      if(distX>0){
        move(-1,0);
      }
      else{
        move(1,0);
      }
    }
    else{
      if(distY>0){
        move(0,1);
      }
      else{
        move(0,-1);
      }
    }
  }
}
```

A valid swipe is detected each time the move function is called.

This is the move function:

```
function move(deltaX,deltaY){
  switch(level[playerPosition.y+deltaY][playerPosition.x+deltaX]){
    case 0:
    case 2:
    level[playerPosition.y][playerPosition.x]-=4;
    playerPosition.x+=deltaX;
    playerPosition.y+=deltaY;
    level[playerPosition.y][playerPosition.x]+=4;
    playerSprite.setPosition(165+25*playerPosition.x,185-
25*playerPosition.y);
    break;
    case 3:
    case 5:
    if(level[playerPosition.y+deltaY*2][playerPosition.x+deltaX*2]==0
|| level[playerPosition.y+deltaY*2][playerPosition.x+deltaX*2]==2){
      level[playerPosition.y][playerPosition.x]-=4;
      playerPosition.x+=deltaX;
      playerPosition.y+=deltaY;
      level[playerPosition.y][playerPosition.x]+=1;
      playerSprite.setPosition(165+25*playerPosition.x,185-
25*playerPosition.y);
      level[playerPosition.y+deltaY][playerPosition.x+deltaX]+=3;
      var movingCrate = cratesArray[playerPosition.y]
[playerPosition.x];
      movingCrate.setPosition(movingCrate.getPosition().
x+25*deltaX,movingCrate.getPosition().y-25*deltaY);
      cratesArray[playerPosition.y+deltaY][playerPosition.
x+deltaX]=movingCrate;
      cratesArray[playerPosition.y][playerPosition.x]=null;
    }
    break;
  }
}
```

Enjoy your game.

# Summary

In this chapter, you learned how to use sprite sheets to manage your assets, create pixel-perfect games, and detect swipes. You also created a great puzzle game called Cocosban.

If you noticed, player and crate movements are made by making assets jump to their destination. Why don't you add a tween to create a smooth movement? It would be a great achievement for you to do it.

Also, there's no check to see whether the player completed the level. A completed level has no crates outside crate goals. Try to develop it.

Then, follow me through a path full of music; we will add sound effects to our games!

# 5
# Become a Musical Maestro

Although you might think the games you created while reading this book are complete, they lack some kind of atmosphere due to a simple reason: they are mute.

No sounds, no background music, nothing. A complete, fully polished game must have background music and sound effects, and that's what you are going to learn in this chapter.

Follow me, and you will be able to:

- Add sound effects to your games
- Add background music to your games
- Loop sounds
- Start and stop sounds
- Changing the volume of music and sound effects

Also, just because the more you learn the better it is, you will also see how to create option menus.

Now, surf the Web and choose some great music and sound effects.

## Choosing sounds

Let's guess what happened. You found that incredible song, which is a mix between electronic and heavy metal and think it would fit really good in your space shooter game. You downloaded it and enjoyed 4 minutes and 56 seconds of Blu-ray quality sound.

Also, in a matter of minutes, you found at least three more songs that would also fit perfectly in your game. Let's add them all, doing an in-game radio like in a GTA series.

No. Wait! The player is running your game in a browser, probably outside any free Wi-Fi zone, with a not so high download speed. You simply can't make them wait half an hour just to download a song unless your name is Lady Gaga and that sound is your latest smash hit.

People want to press *play* and play your game; remember, you are making games, not sounds in a matter of seconds, so choose your sounds wisely, they can't be bigger than the game itself.

Play with sound quality until you find a good compromise between quality and weight, and when choosing background music, a short loop is way better than a long tune.

Also, remember different browsers in different operative system read different sound types, so you should provide the same sound in three different formats: MP3, WAV, and OGG.

 Talking about sounds optimization and conversion is beyond the scope of this book, but I suggest you use the free software I used to edit sounds to be included in my games, **Audacity**, found at http://audacity.sourceforge.net/.

# Preloading sounds

Preloading sounds is exactly the same as preloading graphic assets. In the assets folder, there are two mp3 files: loop.mp3, which is a short loop used as background music, and bang.mp3, which is an Uzi sound effect. Remember in your final project, you will have to include the WAV and OGG files as well in order to ensure the largest compatibility possible among different browsers in various devices.

The loadassets.js file will include the array of sounds to preload:

```
var gameResources = [
  "assets/bang.mp3",
  "assets/loop.mp3"
];
```

Now, let's create a menu to play with sounds and music.

# Creating a sound menu

There are several ways to create a menu, and the most interesting is to create the graphic assets of every menu item, then add touch or mouse listeners, and handle the whole thing in a way you should already know.

This time, you'll see something new: the Cocos2d-JS built-in `Menu` class.

This is the content of `gameScript.js`:

```
var gameScene = cc.Scene.extend({
  onEnter:function () {
    this._super();
    gameLayer = new game();
    gameLayer.init();
    this.addChild(gameLayer);
  }
});

var game = cc.Layer.extend({
  init:function () {
    this._super();
    this.audioEngine = cc.audioEngine;
    var playSoundMenu = new cc.MenuItemFont.create("Play Sound
effect",this.playSound,this);
    playSoundMenu.setPosition(new cc.Point(0,350));
    var playBGMusicMenu = new cc.MenuItemFont.create("Play BG
music",this.playBGMusic,this);
    playBGMusicMenu.setPosition(new cc.Point(0,300));
    var stopBGMusicMenu = new cc.MenuItemFont.create("Stop BG
music",this.stopBGMusic,this);
    stopBGMusicMenu.setPosition(new cc.Point(0,250));
    var musicUpMenu = new cc.MenuItemFont.create("Music volume
Up",this.musicUp,this);
    musicUpMenu.setPosition(new cc.Point(0,200));
    var musicDownMenu = new cc.MenuItemFont.create("Music volume
Down",this.musicDown,this);
    musicDownMenu.setPosition(new cc.Point(0,150));
    var effectsUpMenu = new cc.MenuItemFont.create("Effects volume
Up",this.effectsUp,this);
```

```
    effectsUpMenu.setPosition(new cc.Point(0,100));
    var effectsDownMenu = new cc.MenuItemFont.create("Effects volume
Down",this.effectsDown,this);
    effectsDownMenu.setPosition(new cc.Point(0,50));
    var menu = cc.Menu.create(playSoundMenu,playBGMusicMenu,stopBGMusi
cMenu,musicUpMenu,musicDownMenu,effectsUpMenu,effectsDownMenu);
    menu.setPosition(new cc.Point(160,40));
    this.addChild(menu);
    }
});
```

That's really a lot of stuff, but there isn't that much to learn: the `gameScene` variable declaration is the same as in previous projects, and the game declaration is different from the following line of code:

```
this.audioEngine = cc.audioEngine;
```

This will allow you to initialize the audio engine, you only find a lot: seven menu item declarations to be precise like this one:

```
var playSoundMenu = new cc.MenuItemFont.create("Play Sound
effect",this.playSound,this);
playSoundMenu.setPosition(new cc.Point(0,350));
```

The `cc.MenuItemFont.create` function creates a text menu item with a zoom effect when it's clicked.

The three arguments represent the text to display, the callback function to run, and the target to run the callback, respectively.

All seven menu items are created in the same way and placed with the `setPosition` method you already know.

Once all these items have been created, you turn them into an actual menu with the following code snippet:

```
var menu = cc.Menu.create
(playSoundMenu,playBGMusicMenu,stopBGMusicMenu,musicUpMenu,musicDownMe
nu,effectsUpMenu,effectsDownMenu);
menu.setPosition(new cc.Point(160,40));
this.addChild(menu);
```

The `Menu.create` function contains all the menu items you just created, and it's added and positioned on the stage as usual with `addChild` and `setPosition`.

Run the project and you will see what is shown in the following screenshot:

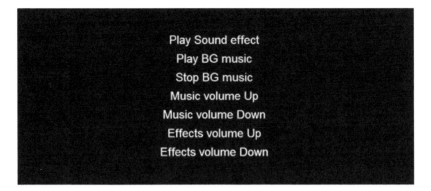

Click or touch the menu items to see the zoom-in effect, although nothing happens because callback functions still have to be created.

# Managing music and sound effects

It's time to create all the callback functions, so let's expand the content of the game class declaration:

```
var game = cc.Layer.extend({
  init:function () {
    // same as before
  },
  playSound:function(){
    this.audioEngine.playEffect("assets/bang.mp3");
  },
  playBGMusic:function(){
    if(!this.audioEngine.isMusicPlaying()){
      this.audioEngine.playMusic("assets/loop.mp3",true);
    }
  },
  stopBGMusic:function(){
    if(this.audioEngine.isMusicPlaying()){
      this.audioEngine.stopMusic();
    }
  },
  musicUp:function(){
    this.audioEngine.setMusicVolume(this.audioEngine.
getMusicVolume()+0.1);
```

```
    },
    musicDown:function(){
        this.audioEngine.setMusicVolume(this.audioEngine.
getMusicVolume()-0.1);
    },
    effectsUp:function(){
        this.audioEngine.setEffectsVolume(this.audioEngine.
getEffectsVolume()+0.1);
    },
    effectsDown:function(){
        this.audioEngine.setEffectsVolume(this.audioEngine.
getEffectsVolume()-0.1);
    }
});
```

Now, if you test the project, you will be able to play and stop sounds as well as adjust adjust the volume of the music and sound effects.

Let's see all the functions one by one:

```
playSound:function(){
    this.audioEngine.playEffect("assets/bang.mp3");
}
playEffect method simply plays a sound effect.
playBGMusic:function(){
    if(!this.audioEngine.isMusicPlaying()){
        this.audioEngine.playMusic("assets/loop.mp3",true);
    }
}
```

When the music is not playing, use the `playMusic` method to play the music. The second argument means to loop it. You can see whether the music is playing, thanks to the `isMusicPlaying` method:

```
stopBGMusic:function(){
    if(this.audioEngine.isMusicPlaying()){
        this.audioEngine.stopMusic();
    }
}
```

Applying the same concept used before, if the music is already playing, you stop it with the `stopMusic` method:

```
musicUp:function(){
   this.audioEngine.setMusicVolume
(this.audioEngine.getMusicVolume()+0.1);
}
```

The `getMusicVolume` and `setMusicVolume` methods get and set music volume with values from 0 (no volume) to 1 (full volume), respectively:

```
musicDown:function(){
this.audioEngine.setMusicVolume(this.audioEngine.
getMusicVolume()-0.1);
}
```

The following concepts are applied to `getEffectsVolume` and `setEffectsVolume`:

```
effectsUp:function(){
   this.audioEngine.setEffectsVolume
(this.audioEngine.getEffectsVolume()+0.1);
}
effectsDown:function(){
   this.audioEngine.setEffectsVolume
(this.audioEngine.getEffectsVolume()-0.1);
}
```

Also, this is how you can manage sounds with Cocos2d-JS.

# Summary

Thanks to what you learned in this chapter, your games will now feature background music and sound effects.

Why don't you add sounds to the games you made during previous chapters? Then, get ready because we are going to bring interactivity to a whole new level!

# 6

# Controlling the Game with Virtual Pads

One of the most important things to consider when making a cross-platform game is the way the player will control the main character. Most of the devices your game will be running on won't have a keyboard or a mouse, and although more and more portable devices now support pads, your game must also be playable without pads.

In this chapter, I will show you three of the most popular ways to create virtual pads on any device. Among other things, you will learn how to:

- Scroll big images to give an idea of an endless background
- Schedule events
- Control the frame rate
- Check collision between sprites
- Create a simple particle system
- Move sprites manually or using actions

So, the first thing to do is take a look at how successful games allow players to interact with them using virtual pads.

# Overview of virtual pads

The oldest, simplest, and highly discouraged way to create virtual pads is placing directional buttons on the screen and controlling the character according to the button pressed by the player.

I also used this kind of virtual pad in the first version of my *Sokoban* game before I made the game playable with swipes, as I showed you during the creation of *Cocosban* game.

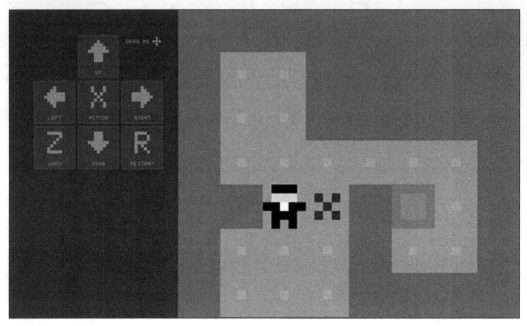

The Sokoban game

In this game, you move the character by clicking or tapping exactly on an arrow button. It can fit in a slow-paced puzzle game, but becomes unplayable in a fast-paced arcade.

That's why famous platform games such as *Mikey Shorts* use ghost buttons. Ghost buttons act like normal buttons, but the sensible area is way bigger than the icon itself.

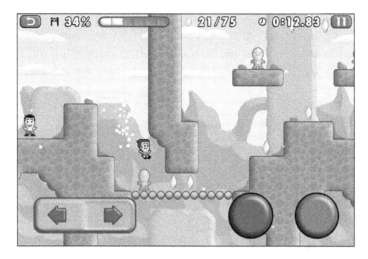

Although the buttons aren't bigger than the ones used in my *Sokoban* game, the sensible area covers the entire screen: the actual red button sensible area is the whole column of the screen covering the red button icon, the blue button sensible area is the whole column of the screen covering the blue button icon, and so on.

Another way to handle virtual pads is by using the virtual analogic pad. Although, the way to control *Mikey Shorts* is digital, which means one button can only be pressed or released; sometimes, games require more precision in movements like the following screenshot of the *Grand Theft Auto* series:

On the bottom left-hand side of the screen, you can see a virtual analogic pad. The pad is initially activated by touching the screen, then the further you drag the pad from its original position, the faster the character will walk or run.

Another way to create virtual pads that I would like to mention is the one used in the *VVVVVV* game, which does not show any icon. A screenshot of the *VVVVVV* game is shown as follows:

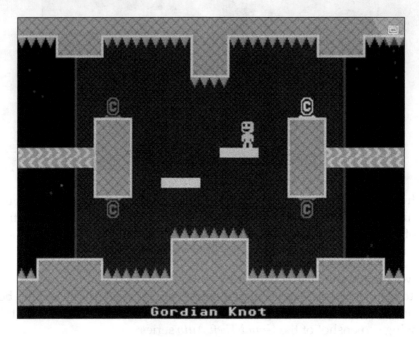

You simply move the character left and right by continuously dragging, or dragging and holding your finger on the device, and I have to say it works way better than the old virtual pad because you can virtually use any spot on the device to move. Above all, there isn't any *origin* you have to cross to change direction: no matter how far you move your finger from the point you start touching, once you move the finger in the opposite direction, the character will walk in the other direction.

Now, apart from the first example, which I said is obsolete, you will see how to create all these ways to control your character with virtual pads.

# First things first – the game

We are making a little game just to test our virtual pads: a landscape game with a shopping cart surrounded by falling bombs and strawberries trying to catch strawberries while avoiding bombs? Does it sound crazy? It is.

This is the content of our `assets` folder:

The making of the entire game is very similar to the making of the endless space runner, so there's no need to talk about code you should already know.

This is the content of `main.js`:

```
cc.game.onStart = function(){
  var screenSize = cc.view.getFrameSize();
  cc.view.setDesignResolutionSize(480, 320, cc.ResolutionPolicy.SHOW_
ALL);
  cc.LoaderScene.preload(gameResources, function () {
    cc.director.runScene(new gameScene());
  }, this);
};
cc.game.run();
```

Just look at the resolution policy to make the game work in landscape mode.

This is the content of `loadassets.js`:

```
var gameResources = [
  "assets/bomb.png",
  "assets/cart.png",
  "assets/strawberry.png",
  "assets/leftbutton.png",
  "assets/rightbutton.png"
];
```

The content of `gamescript.js`, as said, is very similar to the content of the endless space runner.

First, let's take a look at the final result:

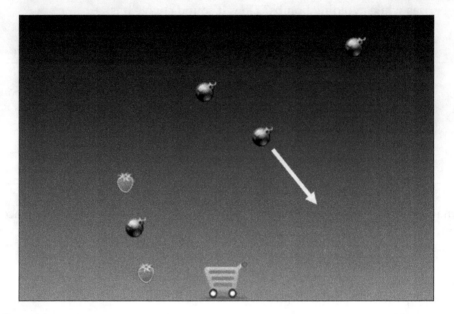

We have a cart in the bottom center of the stage, and fruit and bombs falling every second with a random trajectory.

As I already told you, there's nothing new! You should know everything you need to build this game. This is `gamescript.js`: first, you need two global variables to handle the cart itself and the layer that will be filled with fruit and bombs:

```
var itemsLayer;
var cart;
```

The `gameScene` is then defined as usual:

```
var gameScene = cc.Scene.extend({
  onEnter:function () {
    this._super();
    gameLayer = new game();
    gameLayer.init();
    this.addChild(gameLayer);
  }
});
```

The `game` class declaration contains the core of the game itself:

```
var game = cc.Layer.extend({
  init:function () {
    this._super();
    var backgroundLayer = cc.LayerGradient.create(cc.color(0,0,0,255),
cc.color(0x46,0x82,0xB4,255));
    this.addChild(backgroundLayer);
    itemsLayer = cc.Layer.create()
    this.addChild(itemsLayer)
    topLayer = cc.Layer.create()
    this.addChild(topLayer)
    cart = cc.Sprite.create("assets/cart.png");
    topLayer.addChild(cart,0);
    cart.setPosition(240,24);
    this.schedule(this.addItem,1);
  },
  addItem:function(){
    var item = new Item();
    itemsLayer.addChild(item,1);
  },
  removeItem:function(item){
    itemsLayer.removeChild(item);
  }
});
```

This looks like it's a lot of code, but there's nothing new: we simply add a background gradient, then two layers: one for fruit and bombs and one for the cart, and finally, we add the cart itself. To create fruit and bombs, we use the `schedule` method, which calls the `addItem` function every second to create a new `Item` class instance, while the `removeItem` function will remove fruit and bombs once they fly off the screen.

This is really similar to the creation of the space endless runner, and the same goes for the creation of fruit and bombs in the `Item` declaration:

```
var Item = cc.Sprite.extend({
  ctor:function() {
    this._super();
    if(Math.random()<0.5){
      this.initWithFile("assets/bomb.png");
      this.isBomb=true;
    }
    else{
      this.initWithFile("assets/strawberry.png");
```

```
            this.isBomb=false;
        }
    },
    onEnter:function() {
        this._super();
        this.setPosition(Math.random()*400+40,350);
        var moveAction = cc.MoveTo.create(8, new cc.Point(Math.
random()*400+40,-50));
        this.runAction(moveAction);
        this.scheduleUpdate();
    },
    update:function(dt){
        if(this.getPosition().y<35 && this.getPosition().y>30 && Math.
abs(this.getPosition().x-cart.getPosition().x)<10 && !this.isBomb){
            gameLayer.removeItem(this);
            console.log("FRUIT");
        }
        if(this.getPosition().y<35 && Math.abs(this.getPosition().x-cart.
getPosition().x)<25 && this.isBomb){
            gameLayer.removeItem(this);
            console.log("BOMB");
        }
        if(this.getPosition().y<-30){
            gameLayer.removeItem(this)
        }
    }
});
```

Again, there's a lot of code, but most of it is pure JavaScript and has nothing to do with Cocos2d-JS. Let's take a look at it anyway:

```
ctor:function() {
    this._super();
    if(Math.random()<0.5){
        this.initWithFile("assets/bomb.png");
        this.isBomb=true;
    }
    else{
        this.initWithFile("assets/strawberry.png");
        this.isBomb=false;
    }
}
```

How can you decide whether the current item will be a fruit or a bomb? By simply drawing a random number, then according to its value, use the bomb or fruit image. The `isBomb` custom attribute will tell us whether it's a bomb (`true`) or a fruit (`false`):

```
onEnter:function() {
  this._super();
  this.setPosition(Math.random()*400+40,350);
  var moveAction = cc.MoveTo.create(8, new cc.Point(Math.
random()*400+40,-50));
  this.runAction(moveAction);
  this.scheduleUpdate();
}
```

When it's time to place it on the stage, we put it in a random horizontal position outside the top of the screen and create a tween to move it outside the bottom of the screen in a different random horizontal position. Pretty similar to the endless runner's asteroid movement.

```
update:function(dt){
  if(this.getPosition().y<35 && this.getPosition().y>30 && Math.
abs(this.getPosition().x-cart.getPosition().x)<10 && !this.isBomb){
    gameLayer.removeItem(this);
    console.log("FRUIT");
  }
  if(this.getPosition().y<35 && Math.abs(this.getPosition().x-cart.
getPosition().x)<25 && this.isBomb){
    gameLayer.removeItem(this);
    console.log("BOMB");
  }
  if(this.getPosition().y<-30){
    gameLayer.removeItem(this)
  }
}
```

The `update` function ,which is called at every frame, checks for three conditions:

1.  If the item is a fruit and it's very close to the cart, then we remove the item and output some text to the console to have a debug message, which displays the player hit a fruit.

2.  If the item is a bomb and it's close (not as close as required by the fruit), but close to the cart, then we remove the item and output some text to the console to get a debug message, which displays the player hit a bomb. This is a difficult game, because being hit by a bomb is easier than collecting a fruit.

3.   If the item (no matter which kind of item) is outside the bottom of the stage, we need to remove it.

That's all for the game. Now, you need to let the player control the cart in the three ways mentioned before.

# Controlling the cart with ghost buttons

To control the cart with ghost buttons, first, you have to place the button on the screen, which, as said, will only act as a fake button because the entire left and right area of the stage will represent the actual button.

You need to add some global variables to the script to handle left and right buttons as well as the horizontal speed:

```
var itemsLayer;
var cart;
var xSpeed = 0;
var left;
var right;
```

The xSpeed variable represents the horizontal speed of the cart, while the left and right variables will be assigned to left and right arrow buttons.

Now, the init function needs to place the buttons, set the touch listener, and schedule the update at each frame:

```
init:function () {
   this._super();
   var backgroundLayer = cc.LayerGradient.create(cc.color(0,0,0,255),
cc.color(0x46,0x82,0xB4,255));
   this.addChild(backgroundLayer);
   itemsLayer = cc.Layer.create()
   this.addChild(itemsLayer)
   topLayer = cc.Layer.create()
   this.addChild(topLayer)
   cart = cc.Sprite.create("assets/cart.png");
   topLayer.addChild(cart,0);
   cart.setPosition(240,24);
   left = cc.Sprite.create("assets/leftbutton.png");
   topLayer.addChild(left,0);
```

```
    left.setPosition(40,160)
    left.setOpacity(128)
    right = cc.Sprite.create("assets/rightbutton.png");
    topLayer.addChild(right,0);
    right.setPosition(440,160);
    right.setOpacity(128)
    this.schedule(this.addItem,1);
    cc.eventManager.addListener(touchListener, this);
    this.scheduleUpdate();
}
```

I would like you to check whether both left and right arrow buttons are placed on the `topLayer` and their opacity is set to half transparent. Also, look at the name of the listener variable we are going to create: `touchListener`.

Also, this is the `touchListener` declaration:

```
var touchListener = cc.EventListener.create({
    event: cc.EventListener.TOUCH_ONE_BY_ONE,
    swallowTouches: true,
    onTouchBegan: function (touch, event) {
      if(touch.getLocation().x < 240){
        xSpeed = -2;
        left.setOpacity(255);
        right.setOpacity(128);
      }
      else{
        xSpeed = 2;
        right.setOpacity(255);
        left.setOpacity(128);
      }
      return true;
    },
    onTouchEnded:function (touch, event) {
      xSpeed = 0;
      left.setOpacity(128);
      right.setOpacity(128);
    }
})
```

It's a touch event like the ones we've met before. Let's take a closer look at the triggered events:

```
onTouchBegan: function (touch, event) {
    if(touch.getLocation().x < 240){
        xSpeed = -2;
        left.setOpacity(255);
        right.setOpacity(128);
    }
    else{
        xSpeed = 2;
        right.setOpacity(255);
        left.setOpacity(128);
    }
    return true;
}
```

When the player touches the screen that deals with ghost buttons, we only need to check whether the left or right portion of the screen has been touched, set xSpeed accordingly as well as turn the speed to on or off, and set it at full or half opacity to the respective arrow buttons.

It's very important that the function returns true if you want Cocos2d-JS to be able to check when the player stops touching the screen. To acheive this, add the following code snippet:

```
onTouchEnded:function (touch, event) {
    xSpeed = 0;
    left.setOpacity(128);
    right.setOpacity(128);
}
```

When the player stops touching the screen, xSpeed is set back to zero and both buttons are turned off.

Now, you only have to move the cart in the update function of the game class:

```
update:function(dt){
    if(xSpeed>0){
        cart.setFlippedX(true);
    }
    if(xSpeed<0){
        cart.setFlippedX(false);
```

```
    }
    cart.setPosition(cart.getPosition().
        x+xSpeed,cart.getPosition().y);
    }
```

There's really no need to explain anything as you are only moving the cart by xSpeed pixels; just take a look at the setFlippedX method to flip the cart horizontally when it's going right.

Run the game and you will see what is shown in the following screenshot:

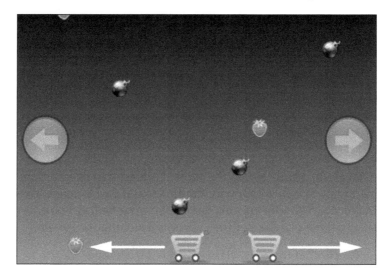

Touch the screen anywhere to move the cart to the left or to the right according to the position of the screen you are touching. That's all about ghost buttons. Now, let's see how to control the game using the virtual pad.

# Controlling the cart with a virtual pad

The first thing to do in order to control a game with a virtual pad is to have a virtual pad. So we need to change some images in our assets folder:

The left and right buttons have been removed to be replaced by virtual pad images, so `loadassets.js` changes this way:

```
var gameResources = [
   "assets/bomb.png",
   "assets/cart.png",
   "assets/strawberry.png",
   "assets/touchorigin.png",
   "assets/touchend.png"
];
```

Obviously, most of the game remains the same because you are only changing the way you control the cart. You need to change the global variables a bit:

```
var itemsLayer;
var cart;
var xSpeed = 0;
var touchOrigin;
var touching = false;
var touchEnd;
```

While game-related variables remain the same, I added two new variables called `touchOrigin` and `touchEnd`, which will handle virtual pad touches. Also, the variables used before to handle buttons have been removed. A Boolean variable called `touching` will tell us whether the player is touching the screen.

Now, the `init` function of the `game` class needs some changes too:

```
init:function () {
   this._super();
   var backgroundLayer = cc.LayerGradient.create(cc.color(0,0,0,255),
cc.color(0x46,0x82,0xB4,255));
   this.addChild(backgroundLayer);
   itemsLayer = cc.Layer.create()
   this.addChild(itemsLayer)
   topLayer = cc.Layer.create()
   this.addChild(topLayer)
   cart = cc.Sprite.create("assets/cart.png");
   topLayer.addChild(cart,0);
   cart.setPosition(240,24);
   this.schedule(this.addItem,1);
   cc.eventManager.addListener(touchListener, this);
   this.scheduleUpdate();
}
```

Basically, all lines about the left and right button have been removed, but the core of the script is in the touchListener declaration:

```
var touchListener = cc.EventListener.create({
  event: cc.EventListener.TOUCH_ONE_BY_ONE,
  swallowTouches: true,
  onTouchBegan: function (touch, event) {
    touchOrigin = cc.Sprite.create("assets/touchorigin.png");
    topLayer.addChild(touchOrigin,0);
    touchOrigin.setPosition(touch.getLocation().x,touch.
getLocation().y);
    touchEnd = cc.Sprite.create("assets/touchend.png");
    topLayer.addChild(touchEnd,0);
    touchEnd.setPosition(touch.getLocation().x,touch.getLocation().y);
    touching = true;
    return true;
  },
  onTouchMoved: function (touch, event) {
    touchEnd.setPosition(touch.getLocation().x,touchEnd.
getPosition().y);
  },
  onTouchEnded:function (touch, event) {
    touching = false;
    topLayer.removeChild(touchOrigin);
    topLayer.removeChild(touchEnd);
  }
})
```

The first thing I would like you to see is the three events:

1.  onTouchBegan: This event places both virtual pad sprites in the touch location and sets the touching Boolean variable to true.

2.  onTouchMoved: This event updates the touchEnd sprite to the current touch position. As the name suggests, this event is triggered when the player moves their finger around the screen.

3.  onTouchEnded: This event removes both virtual pad sprites and sets the touching Boolean variable to false.

It's easy to guess how I am moving the cart in the update function of the game class. If the touching variable is true, the cart speed is the difference between the touchEnd and touchOrigin functions' *x* coordinates:

```
update:function(dt){
  if(touching){
    xSpeed = (touchEnd.getPosition().
      x-touchOrigin.getPosition().x)/50;
    if(xSpeed>0){
      cart.setFlippedX(true);
    }
    if(xSpeed<0){
      cart.setFlippedX(false);
    }
    cart.setPosition(cart.getPosition().
      x+xSpeed,cart.getPosition().y);
  }
}
```

Being an analogic pad, the greater the difference between the touchEnd and touchOrigin functions' *x* coordinates, the faster the cart movement. I divided the difference by 50 to keep the game playable; otherwise, the game would move too fast.

Test the game and play.

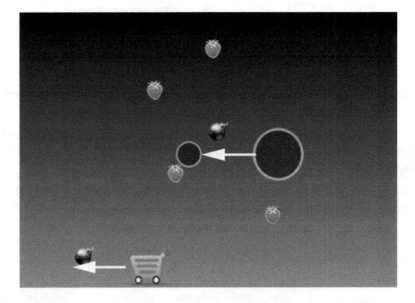

Touch and drag the screen to move the cart at the proper speed. Also, that's all for the analogic virtual pad too.

# Controlling the cart just with your finger

Although you have been controlling the cart with your finger throughout the entire chapter, you have always had visual feedback of your movements. The last way to move the cart that I am going to show in this chapter does not provide any visual feedback, but it works great in games where movements are limited to one axis, such as the one you are making now.

First, you don't need any graphic assets except the ones directly related to the game, so our `loadassets.js` file is smaller than ever:

```
var gameResources = [
"assets/bomb.png",
"assets/cart.png",
"assets/strawberry.png"
];
```

Now, the changes are even smaller than the ones you made when you created the virtual pad from the ghost button: you just need to change the global variables a bit:

```
var itemsLayer;
var xSpeed = 0;
var cart;
var detectedX;
var savedX;
var touching=false;
```

The `detectedX` and `savedX` variables will store the current and last saved finger or mouse in a horizontal position.

The `touchListener` content is way simpler than before because you don't have to manage images:

```
var touchListener = cc.EventListener.create({
  event: cc.EventListener.TOUCH_ONE_BY_ONE,
  swallowTouches: true,
  onTouchBegan: function (touch, event) {
    touching = true;
    detectedX = touch.getLocation().x;
    savedX = detectedX
    return true;
  },
  onTouchMoved: function (touch, event) {
    detectedX = touch.getLocation().x;
  },
```

```
onTouchEnded:function (touch, event) {
   touching = false;
}
})
```

Apart from setting the `touching` Boolean variable to `true` or `false`, as seen before, you play with `detectedX` and `savedX` to store the initial and current touch horizontal coordinate.

The `update` function of the `game` class takes care of the rest:

```
update:function(dt){
   if(touching){
      var deltaX = savedX - detectedX
      if(deltaX>0){
         xSpeed = -2;
      }
      if(deltaX<0){
         xSpeed = 2;
      }
      savedX = detectedX;
      if(xSpeed>0){
         cart.setFlippedX(true);
      }
      if(xSpeed<0){
         cart.setFlippedX(false);
      }
      cart.setPosition(cart.getPosition().
         x+xSpeed,cart.getPosition().y);
   }
}
```

When the player is touching the screen, the difference between current and last saved horizontal touch coordinate is made to see whether the cart has to move to the left or to the right. Then, the last saved horizontal touch coordinate is updated to the current horizontal touch coordinate, which is ready to change again if an `onTouchMoved` event is triggered.

Test the game and move your finger back and forth, you will see the cart change direction as soon as your finger changes direction.

# Summary

Congratulations! This was a hard and long chapter because it explained three different ways to control your games. Now, it's up to you to use the way you think it fits better for each of your games, so why don't you write down a list of your favourite mobile games and think about what kind of way would you use to control the player?

Now, let's move on to the next chapter where you will meet realistic physics.

# 7
# Adding Physics to Your Games Using the Box2D Engine

If you ask me what the biggest revolution in casual gaming is, no doubt I'll say physics engines. A lot of top-selling casual games such as Crayon Physics, Totem Destroyer, Crush the Castle, Angry Birds, Tiny Wings, just to mention a few use physics engines to add a realistic behavior that wouldn't be possible without such engines.

The most popular among physics engines in the 2D world is Box2D, initially written in C++, then ported to all major languages, including JavaScript.

Cocos2d-JS supports Box2D, and this chapter will cover the creation of a physics game, including these concepts:

- Configuring and setting up Cocos2d-JS to add the Box2D engine to your games
- Creating a physics world
- Giving the world a realistic gravity
- Combining bodies, shapes, and fixtures to create a physics object
- Creating a material
- Creating static objects
- Creating dynamic objects
- Attaching sprites to physics objects
- Selecting physics objects with the mouse/finger
- Destroying physics objects
- Checking for collisions among objects
- Running the physics simulation

That's a lot of stuff, isn't it?

By the end of the chapter, you will have a playable level of a famous physics game.

# Before you start

Learning Box2D in just a few pages is not possible. A whole book is what you will need to start mastering it.

> For an in-depth understanding of Box2D, you can find my book, *Box2D for Flash Games*, at https://www.packtpub.com/ game-development/box2d-flash-games.

Anyway, this chapter will give you the bare bones to add physics to your games. Although experienced Box2D users may find some concepts such as collision detection covered in a less-than-perfect way, in the end, it works and that's what really matters in the scope of this chapter: giving you the knowledge to start learning Box2D and include it into your Cocos2d-JS projects.

# Adding the Box2D engine to your project

The best game to write for you to learn most Box2D concepts is Totem Destroyer. It can be found at http://armorgames.com/play/1871/totem-destroyer.

You have to smash bricks by clicking/tapping on them while being careful not to let the totem fall to the ground, or it's game over. Not all bricks can be destroyed. In the level shown in the following screenshot, dark bricks can't be destroyed:

Although the game has quite a simple gameplay, it features some advanced physics concepts, such as collision detection and how to select a physics body.

We will build this level; so, as usual, the first thing we need to do is take care of the content of the assets folder:

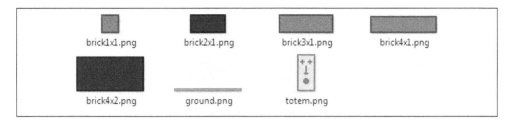

And this is the content of `loadassets.js`:

```
var gameResources = [
  "assets/brick1x1.png",
  "assets/brick2x1.png",
  "assets/brick3x1.png",
  "assets/brick4x1.png",
  "assets/brick4x2.png",
  "assets/ground.png",
  "assets/totem.png"
];
```

To keep loading times as fast as possible, the basic Cocos2d-JS source we used in the previous chapters did not feature any physics engine.

In order to have Cocos2d-JS work with Box2D, we have to load another module called `external`, which we will define in the `project.json` file:

```
{
  "debugMode" : 0,
  "showFPS" : false,
  "frameRate" : 60,
  "id" : "gameCanvas",
  "renderMode" : 0,
  "engineDir":"cocos2d-html5/",

  "modules" : ["cocos2d","external"],

  "jsList" : [
    "src/loadassets.js",
    "src/gamescript.js"
    ]
}
```

Now, the engine knows we will use Box2D; so, we can focus on the game itself.

# Configuring the physics world

From now on, all the script will be written in `gamescript.js` as usual, so be prepared to write your first Cocos2d-JS Box2D script.

Some of the magic happens from the first two lines, which declare global variables:

```
var world;
var worldScale = 30;
```

Here, the `world` variable will represent the physics world we are setting the game in, and will include its own gravity and other properties that we will discover. However, first I want to say a couple of words about `worldScale`.

Box2D is a realistic physics engine that uses real-world units of measurement. This way, everything you will create in Box2D world will be measured in meters. If you create a box whose side length is 2, you mean it's two meters.

On the other hand, browsers have their own unit of measurement, which is pixels. You can have a game 480 pixels wide, but you'll never find a game two meters wide.

So, we need to find a ratio between pixels and meters. In almost every project, the *1 meter = 30 pixels* setting works fine and allows us to think and work in pixels without caring about the Box2D internal unit of measurement.

The `gameScene` class declaration does not change:

```
var gameScene = cc.Scene.extend({
  onEnter:function () {
    this._super();
    gameLayer = new game();
    gameLayer.init();
    this.addChild(gameLayer);
  }
});
```

The interesting part as usual can be found in the `game` declaration:

```
var game = cc.Layer.extend({
  init:function () {
    this._super();
    var backgroundLayer = cc.LayerGradient.create(cc.
color(0xdf,0x9f,0x83,255), cc.color(0xfa,0xf7,0x9f,255));
    this.addChild(backgroundLayer);
```

```
    var gravity = new Box2D.Common.Math.b2Vec2(0, -10)
    world = new Box2D.Dynamics.b2World(gravity, true);

    this.scheduleUpdate();
  },
  update:function(dt){
    world.Step(dt,10,10);
    console.log(world);
  }
});
```

Once you run the project, in your console, you should see a several instances of **b2World**.

This means our Box2D physics world is running; let's see what happened.

First, we added a gradient background layer:

```
var backgroundLayer = cc.LayerGradient.create(cc.
color(0xdf,0x9f,0x83,255), cc.color(0xfa,0xf7,0x9f,255));
this.addChild(backgroundLayer);
```

Then, we already know that a physics world has gravity. Here is how we define the gravity:

```
var gravity = new Box2D.Common.Math.b2Vec2(0, -10);
```

All in all, the gravity in the real world can be represented by a vector, and Earth gravity can be represented by a vector (0,9.81), where 9.81 is expressed in meters per second squared, which is the average acceleration of a falling body near the surface of the Earth.

In Box2D, the b2Vec2 type is used to store vectors; while it's clear that we can approximate 9.81 to 10, it's quite unclear why the gravity vector has its *y* value to -10. A negative gravity?

Let me explain: you already know Cocos2d-JS has its origin coordinate in the bottom left of the stage; so, as long as you move from bottom to top, your y coordinate increases. On the other hand, Box2D works in the opposite way: as long as a physics body falls down; its *y* coordinate increases, and setting the gravity at (0,10) would make Cocos2d-JS sprites fly away rather than fall down.

That's why we need to reverse the gravity. In Box2D, internal world bodies will fly away, but what we'll see on the stage are the same objects falling down.

Now, we are finally able to create the world:

```
world = new Box2D.Dynamics.b2World(gravity, true);
```

As you can see, the world has two arguments: the `gravity` variable we created before, and a Boolean flag to determine whether bodies can sleep. Normally, to save CPU time, physics bodies that don't receive hits and aren't affected by forces for some amount of time are put to sleep. This means they still exist in the Box2D world although their position isn't updated at each frame until they wake up because of some event such as a collision or a force applied to them.

The remaining line should already be clear for you. We are enabling the game to schedule the update function to be executed at each frame:

```
this.scheduleUpdate();
```

When we call `scheduleUpdate`, we also need an `update` function, which in this case only contains:

```
world.Step(dt,10,10)
```

The `Step` method advances the simulation for a certain amount of time, `dt` in this case and to be as accurate as possible, while the other two arguments represent the velocity and position iterations, respectively.

These two arguments are needed because most Box2D code is used for an operation called constraint solver, an algorithm that solves all the constraints in the simulation, one at a time. While one single constraint can be easily solved, when more constraints come into play, solving one of them means slightly disrupting the others. That's why we need more iterations in order to have an accurate simulation. The official Box2D documentation suggests you set eight for velocity and three for position, although I usually set both to 10 and do not have any problem in making simple games.

Now, it's time to build the totem.

# Adding bodies to the world

A physics object in the Box2D world is called a body. So, we will see how to add a body to the world. Moreover, since all bodies in our Totem Destroyer game are boxes, we will define a function to create a body and customize it to fit our needs.

We'll start from the end, calling a function we haven't written yet, just to have a look at all arguments that we need to create any kind of body used in Totem Destroyer.

So, the game's `init` function will be modified this way:

```
init:function () {
  this._super();
  var backgroundLayer = cc.LayerGradient.create(cc.
color(0xdf,0x9f,0x83,255), cc.color(0xfa,0xf7,0x9f,255));
  this.addChild(backgroundLayer);
  var gravity = new Box2D.Common.Math.b2Vec2(0, -10)
  world = new Box2D.Dynamics.b2World(gravity, true);

  this.scheduleUpdate();
  this.addBody(240,10,480,20,false,"assets/ground.png","ground");
}
```

Our custom function is called `addBody` and according to the number of arguments will do a lot of things. Let's have a look at the following arguements:

- `240`: This is the horizontal centre of the body, in pixels.

- `10`: This is the vertical centre of the body, in pixels.

- `480`: This is the body width, in pixels.

- `20`: This is the body height, in pixels.

- `false`: This Boolean value determines whether the body is dynamic or not. We are building two kinds of bodies, dynamic bodies, which are affected by forces such as gravity and react to collisions, and static bodies, which can't be moved. This will be a static body.

- `"assets/ground.png"`: These are the graphic assets to be bound to the body.

- `"ground"`: This is the body type. We call it `ground` because it will represent the ground.

So, in other words, we are creating a static body in the bottom of the stage, which will represent the ground.

Now, it is time to see how to create and configure a body with Cocos2d-JS and Box2D. Add the addBody function to the game class:

```
addBody: function
    (posX,posY,width,height,isDynamic,spriteImage,type){
  var fixtureDef = new  Box2D.Dynamics.b2FixtureDef;
  fixtureDef.density = 1.0;
  fixtureDef.friction = 0.5;
  fixtureDef.restitution = 0.2;
  fixtureDef.shape = new Box2D.Collision.Shapes.b2PolygonShape;
  fixtureDef.shape.SetAsBox(0.5*width/worldScale,0.5*height/
worldScale);
  var bodyDef = new Box2D.Dynamics.b2BodyDef;
  if(isDynamic){
    bodyDef.type = Box2D.Dynamics.b2Body.b2_dynamicBody;
  }
  else{
    bodyDef.type = Box2D.Dynamics.b2Body.b2_staticBody;
  }
  bodyDef.position.Set(posX/worldScale,posY/worldScale);
  var userSprite = cc.Sprite.create(spriteImage);
  this.addChild(userSprite, 0);
  userSprite.setPosition(posX,posY);
  bodyDef.userData = {
    type: type,
    asset: userSprite
  }
  var body = world.CreateBody(bodyDef)
  body.CreateFixture(fixtureDef);
}
```

There's a lot of new stuff here, so we will see it line by line. First, we have to create a fixture:

```
var fixtureDef = new  Box2D.Dynamics.b2FixtureDef;
```

Think about a fixture as a relationship between a body, which is the physics actor, and its shape, which determines how the body looks—like a box, like a circle, and so on.

The fixture also determines the material of the body, thanks to these three attributes:

```
fixtureDef.density = 1.0;
fixtureDef.friction = 0.5;
fixtureDef.restitution = 0.2;
```

The `density` attribute affects the mass of the body, `friction` determines how bodies slide along each other, and `restitution` is used to see how a body bounces.

Now, it's time to create the shape attached to the fixture:

```
fixtureDef.shape = new Box2D.Collision.Shapes.b2PolygonShape;
fixtureDef.shape.SetAsBox(0.5*width/worldScale,0.5*height/worldScale);
```

The `SetAsBox` method creates a box given a width and a height that Box2D accepts as half of the actual width and height. So, if you want a box with a width of 30 meters, you'll have to set its width to *30*0.5*. As said, we are talking about pixels so we also have to divide the given width by `worldScale`.

Once we have the shape and the fixture, it's time to care about the physical body:

```
var bodyDef = new Box2D.Dynamics.b2BodyDef;
```

Now, we can say whether the body is static or dynamic. In our game, only the floor will be a static body. The code for this is as follows:

```
if(isDynamic){
  bodyDef.type = Box2D.Dynamics.b2Body.b2_dynamicBody;
}
else{
  bodyDef.type = Box2D.Dynamics.b2Body.b2_staticBody;
}
```

The `type` attribute will determine whether the body will be static or dynamic. Now, we have a shape, a body, and a fixture; why don't we place this body somewhere in the world? See the following code snippet:

```
bodyDef.position.Set(posX/worldScale,posY/worldScale);
```

This can be done with the `position` property. Don't forget the pixels-to-meters conversion.

Now for the hardest part of Box2D. Most of the people trying to learn Box2D fail when it's time to attach a graphic asset to a body. The main reason is, Box2D does not allow you to attach sprites to a body. Print it with a 72-pixel font. You have to manually place sprites on the stage and manually move them as the world updates.

Let's add the sprite:

```
var userSprite = cc.Sprite.create(spriteImage);
this.addChild(userSprite, 0);
userSprite.setPosition(posX,posY);
```

This was easy because we only add a sprite in the same way we have since the start of the first chapter. Anyway, we have to somehow tell Box2D that this sprite belongs to the body we just created.

Too good! There's a `userData` property that we can use to store any kind of custom body information:

```
bodyDef.userData = {
   type: type,
   asset: userSprite
}
```

In this case, I defined an object with the sprites to be linked with and the type of body we are dealing with — in this case, it will be `ground`, according to the argument passed to the `addBody` function.

Finally, we are ready to attach the body to the world, that is, turning our body definition — `b2BodyDef` is a body definition — into a physical body:

```
var body = world.CreateBody(bodyDef);
body.CreateFixture(fixtureDef);
```

The `CreateBody` method will create a real physics body starting from a body definition, while `CreateFixture` will attach a fixture — and its shape — to a body.

Finally, we can run the game and the following image is what you should see:

Finally, we will have a solid ground, and moreover, a function that will allow us to create the entire totem quickly.

Let's add these lines:

```
init:function () {
  this._super();
  var backgroundLayer = cc.LayerGradient.create(cc.
color(0xdf,0x9f,0x83,255), cc.color(0xfa,0xf7,0x9f,255));
  this.addChild(backgroundLayer);
  var gravity = new Box2D.Common.Math.b2Vec2(0, -10)
  world = new Box2D.Dynamics.b2World(gravity, true);

  this.scheduleUpdate();
  this.addBody(240,10,480,20,false,"assets/ground.png","ground");
  this.addBody(204,32,24,24,true,"assets/brick1x1.png",
"destroyable");
  this.addBody(276,32,24,24,true,"assets/brick1x1.png",
  "destroyable");
```

```
    this.addBody(240,56,96,24,true,"assets/brick4x1.png",
"destroyable");
    this.addBody(240,80,48,24,true,"assets/brick2x1.png","solid");
    this.addBody(228,104,72,24,true,"assets/brick3x1.png",
    "destroyable");
    this.addBody(240,140,96,48,true,"assets/brick4x2.png","solid");
    this.addBody(240,188,24,48,true,"assets/totem.png","totem");
}
```

We just have to correctly call the addBody function to have our totem built with each brick defined with its own graphic assets, position, size, and property.

Launch the game now:

That's it! Our totem is standing on the floor, ready to be destroyed.

# Updating sprite position as the world changes

Unfortunately, our totem is still just a bunch of static sprites. Yes, we attached them to a body, but what happens when the world changes?

Try to remove the left foot of the totem, this way:

```
init:function () {
  this._super();
  var backgroundLayer = cc.LayerGradient.create(cc.
color(0xdf,0x9f,0x83,255), cc.color(0xfa,0xf7,0x9f,255));
  this.addChild(backgroundLayer);
  var gravity = new Box2D.Common.Math.b2Vec2(0, -10)
  world = new Box2D.Dynamics.b2World(gravity, true);

  this.scheduleUpdate();
  this.addBody(240,10,480,20,false,"assets/ground.png","ground");
  //this.addBody(204,32,24,24,true,"assets/brick1x1.png",
  "destroyable");
  this.addBody(276,32,24,24,true,"assets/brick1x1.png",
  "destroyable");
  this.addBody(240,56,96,24,true,"assets/brick4x1.png",
  "destroyable");
  this.addBody(240,80,48,24,true,"assets/brick2x1.png","solid");
  this.addBody(228,104,72,24,true,"assets/brick3x1.png",
  "destroyable");
  this.addBody(240,140,96,48,true,"assets/brick4x2.png","solid");
  this.addBody(240,188,24,48,true,"assets/totem.png","totem");
}
```

I just commented a line; let's see what happens:

It definitively looks wrong. The totem should fall!

This happens because we properly placed the sprites when we created the bodies but since then, the sprites' position has not been updated.

The result is the sprites remain in the same position no matter what happens to the bodies. Remember? *Box2D does not allow attaching sprites to a body.* Lesson learned.

We have to move sprites manually, in the `update` function:

```
update:function(dt){
  world.Step(dt,10,10);
  for (var b = world.GetBodyList(); b; b = b.GetNext()) {
    if (b.GetUserData() != null) {
      var mySprite = b.GetUserData().asset;
      mySprite.setPosition(b.GetPosition().x * worldScale,
b.GetPosition().y * worldScale);
      mySprite.setRotation(-1 * cc.radiansToDegrees (b.GetAngle()));
    }
  }
}
```

Run the game now:

Finally, the totem falls! Let's have a look at what happened:

```
for (var b = world.GetBodyList(); b; b = b.GetNext()) {
```

This cycle loops through all bodies placed in the world.

```
if (b.GetUserData() != null) {
```

b is now our current body, and we will see whether we set something into its user data:

```
var mySprite = b.GetUserData().asset;
mySprite.setPosition(b.GetPosition().x * worldScale, b.GetPosition().y
* worldScale);
mySprite.setRotation(-1 * cc.radiansToDegrees (b.GetAngle()));
```

Once we know there's something in the user data, as in this case, we know it's one of the bodies we created to build the totem or the ground. Do you remember we created an object in the user data? The mySprite variable will store the sprite we inserted in this object.

The `GetPosition` method returns body's position; so, we can update the sprite position—remember the conversion from meters to pixels—and `getAngle` returns body rotation.

This way we can manually update all sprites attached to Box2D world bodies.

# Selecting and destroying world bodies

As the name Totem Destroyer suggests, you should be able to destroy the totem. First, uncomment the previously commented line in order to give back the totem its left foot, and then we are ready to destroy bricks when the player touches/clicks them.

Everything starts with a touch, so we have to manage it by first adding the listener to the game's `init` function:

```
init:function () {
    // same as before
    cc.eventManager.addListener(touchListener, this);
}
```

Then create the `listener` variable itself:

```
var touchListener = cc.EventListener.create({
    event: cc.EventListener.TOUCH_ONE_BY_ONE,
    swallowTouches: true,
    onTouchBegan: function (touch, event) {
        var worldPoint = new Box2D.Common.Math.b2Vec2(touch.
getLocation().x/worldScale,touch.getLocation().y/worldScale);
        for (var b = world.GetBodyList(); b; b = b.GetNext()) {
            if (b.GetUserData() != null && b.GetUserData().
type=="destroyable") {
                for(var f = b.GetFixtureList();f; f=f.GetNext()){
                    if(f.TestPoint(worldPoint)){
                        gameLayer.removeChild(b.GetUserData().asset)
                        world.DestroyBody(b);
                    }
                }
            }
        }
    }
});
```

Let's see what we added. First, we have to get click/touch coordinates and translate them into Box2D world coordinates; this means turning pixels into meters and placing coordinates into a `b2Vec2` variable:

```
var worldPoint = new Box2D.Common.Math.b2Vec2(touch.getLocation().x/
    worldScale,touch.getLocation().y/worldScale);
```

Then, we will loop through all bodies in the same way we do when it's time to update the sprite's' position:

```
for (var b = world.GetBodyList(); b; b = b.GetNext()) {
```

Not all bodies can be destroyed: the ground and dark bricks can't be destroyed for instance, so we have to be sure we are only trying to destroy bricks we marked with `destroyable` in their user data:

```
if (b.GetUserData() != null && b.GetUserData().type=="destroyable") {
```

Once we know a brick can be destroyed, we have to loop through all its fixtures and see whether one of them contains the point the player clicked/touched. This is how we will loop through all fixtures of a body:

```
for (var f = b.GetFixtureList();f; f=f.GetNext()){
```

And once `f` represents the current texture, the `TestPoint` method will return `true` if the point passed as an argument is inside the fixture:

```
if(f.TestPoint(worldPoint)){
```

At this time, we are sure the player touched the `b` body and we can destroy it, after having removed the sprite. Remember: *Box2D does not allow you to attach a sprite to a body*. The code snippet for this is shown as follows:

```
gameLayer.removeChild(b.GetUserData().asset);
world.DestroyBody(b);
```

The `DestroyBody` method removes a body from the world.

Run the game and touch some bodies, then you will be able to destroy the light ones.

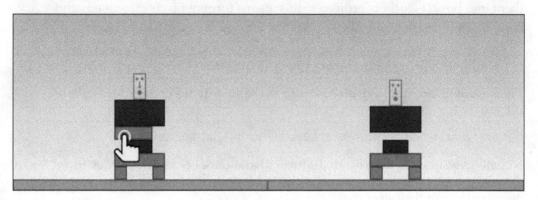

Now the game is ready to be played we only have to check when the idol touches the ground. This is a game-over event, so it's very important.

# Checking for collisions among bodies

To complete the prototype, we need to check whether the idol touches the ground. The simplest way, according to what you have learned about Box2D until now, is to continuously scan through idol collisions and check whether one of the bodies it collides with is the ground.

We need to add some lines to the update function:

```
update:function(dt){
  world.Step(dt,10,10);
  for (var b = world.GetBodyList(); b; b = b.GetNext()) {
    if (b.GetUserData() != null) {
      var mySprite = b.GetUserData().asset;
      mySprite.setPosition(b.GetPosition().x * worldScale,
b.GetPosition().y * worldScale);
      mySprite.setRotation(-1 * cc.radiansToDegrees (b.GetAngle()));
      if(b.GetUserData().type=="totem"){
        for(var c = b.GetContactList(); c; c = c.m_next){
          if(c.other.GetUserData() && c.other.GetUserData().
type=="ground"){
            console.log("Oh no!!!!");
          }
        }
      }
    }
  }
}
```

In the way that we looped through bodies and fixtures, we can loop through contacts using the following line of code:

```
for(var c = b.GetContactList(); c; c = c.m_next){
```

For every `c` contact, we check the body it got in contact with thanks to the `other` property; if its type is `ground`, we output a message in the console. The whole process is made only if the current body is the idol.

Run the game and let the idol touch the ground. You will see several instances of **Oh no!!!!** on your console log. And finally, we have a working Totem Destroyer prototype!!

# Summary

Building a Totem Destroyer level was a great achievement because now you are able to build a cross-platform game like one of the most played browser games; and all thanks to Box2D.

Why don't you improve it by setting a level goal—such as *remove four blocks*—and, when this is achieved, waiting a couple of seconds to see if the idol stays in its position without falling to the ground as in the original game?

# 8
# Adding Physics to Your Games Using the Chipmunk2D Engine

In the previous chapter, you saw how to add physics to your games using Box2D. However, Box2D isn't the only physics engine supported by Cocos2d-JS; you can also feature physics in your games using the Chipmunk2D engine.

So the main question is: should you use Box2D or Chipmunk2D to add physics to your games? There isn't a right answer. Just use the one you feel the most comfortable with.

That's why, in this chapter, I will show you how to create the same Totem Destroyer game using Chipmunk2D, highlighting the similarities and differences between the two physics engines.

As you saw in the previous chapter, it's time to learn:

- Configuring Cocos2d-JS to add Chipmunk2D engine to your games
- Creating a physics space with gravity
- Combining bodies and shapes to create a physics object
- Creating a material
- Creating static objects
- Creating dynamic objects
- Attaching sprites to physics objects

- Selecting physics objects with the mouse or finger
- Destroying physics objects
- Checking for collisions among objects
- Running the physics simulation
- Using debug draw to test your projects

I assume you are quite familiar with basic Box2D concepts discussed in the previous chapter, so I will move on rather fast in the creation of the game.

# Adding the Chipmunk2D engine to your project

As we will create the same game as the one in the previous chapter, I suggest you copy your project into a new folder since we will reuse most of the code already written in the previous chapter. All graphic assets will not change, so simply don't touch the assets folder. The same thing goes for the loadassets.js, main.js and project.json files.

So basically, the only file we will change is gamescript.js. Get ready to dive into the Chipmunk2D world.

## A physics game, without physics

As we already built the Totem Destroyer game prototype, we can strip all the physics parts out of it and leave just the bare bones, where we will build the new physics engine.

The physics-stripped version of gamescript.js is:

```
var gameScene = cc.Scene.extend({
  onEnter:function () {
    this._super();
    gameLayer = new game();
    gameLayer.init();
    this.addChild(gameLayer);
  }
});

var game = cc.Layer.extend({
```

```
    init:function () {
      this._super();
      var backgroundLayer = cc.LayerGradient.create(cc.
color(0xdf,0x9f,0x83,255), cc.color(0xfa,0xf7,0x9f,255));
      this.addChild(backgroundLayer);
      // create physics world somehow
      this.addBody(240,10,480,20,false,"assets/ground.png","ground");
      this.addBody(204,32,24,24,true,"assets/brick1x1.
png","destroyable");
      this.addBody(276,32,24,24,true,"assets/brick1x1.
png","destroyable");
      this.addBody(240,56,96,24,true,"assets/brick4x1.
png","destroyable");
      this.addBody(240,80,48,24,true,"assets/brick2x1.png","solid");
      this.addBody(228,104,72,24,true,"assets/brick3x1.
png","destroyable");
      this.addBody(240,140,96,48,true,"assets/brick4x2.png","solid");
      this.addBody(240,188,24,48,true,"assets/totem.png","totem");
      this.scheduleUpdate();
      cc.eventManager.addListener(touchListener, this);
    },
    addBody: function(posX,posY,width,height,isDynamic,spriteImage,type)
{
      // create the physics body somehow
    },
    update:function(dt){
      // update the world somehow
    }
});

var touchListener = cc.EventListener.create({
    event: cc.EventListener.TOUCH_ONE_BY_ONE,
    onTouchBegan: function (touch, event) {
      // destroy a physics body somehow
    }
})
```

Now, everything is ready to inject Chimpunk2D physics into the game. Let's start from the beginning and create the physics world.

# Configuring the physics space

Look at the heading. It says **Configuring the physics space**. I used *space* rather than *world* because Chipmunk2D calls *space* what Box2D calls *world*.

Both world and space represent the same thing: the place where physics-driven things happen.

Although Chipmunk2D calls it *space*, we will continue to use a variable called *world* to keep as much similarity with Box2D code as we can. This is the best way for you to see the similarities and differences between the two engines.

Change the `init` function in game declaration as follows:

```
init:function () {
  this._super();
  var backgroundLayer = cc.LayerGradient.create(cc.
color(0xdf,0x9f,0x83,255), cc.color(0xfa,0xf7,0x9f,255));
  this.addChild(backgroundLayer);
  world = new cp.Space();
  world.gravity = cp.v(0, -100);
  this.addBody(240,10,480,20,false,"assets/ground.png","ground");
  this.addBody(204,32,24,24,true,"assets/brick1x1.png","destroyable");
  this.addBody(276,32,24,24,true,"assets/brick1x1.png","destroyable");
  this.addBody(240,56,96,24,true,"assets/brick4x1.png","destroyable");
  this.addBody(240,80,48,24,true,"assets/brick2x1.png","solid");
  this.addBody(228,104,72,24,true,"assets/brick3x1.
png","destroyable");
  this.addBody(240,140,96,48,true,"assets/brick4x2.png","solid");
  this.addBody(240,188,24,48,true,"assets/totem.png","totem");
  this.scheduleUpdate();
  cc.eventManager.addListener(touchListener, this);
}
```

Also, create the `world` global variable at the very beginning of the script:

```
var world;
```

Let's see what happens when the following line is executed:

```
world = new cp.Space();
```

The `cp.Space` method creates the Chipmunk2D space; by now, you should know this is the same as the Box2D world:

```
world.gravity = cp.v(0, -100);
```

The gravity property sets world gravity with a vector. cp.v is how Chipmunk2D represents vectors, in the same way as Box2D uses b2Vec2. There's a horizontal and a vertical component and, to simulate earth gravity, you can use (0,-100).

Unlike Box2D, Chipmunk2D does not use real-world units of measurements, so expect to use pixels rather than meters.

# Adding bodies to the space

We already have the addBody function with all required arguments, so it's time to define it:

```
addBody: function(posX,posY,width,height,isDynamic,spriteImage,type){
  if(isDynamic){
    var body = new cp.Body(1,cp.momentForBox(1,width,height));
  }
  else{
    var body = new cp.Body(Infinity,Infinity);
  }
  body.setPos(cp.v(posX,posY));
  if(isDynamic){
    world.addBody(body);
  }
  var shape = new cp.BoxShape(body, width, height);
  shape.setFriction(1);
  shape.setElasticity(0);
  shape.name=type;
  world.addShape(shape);
}
```

This is where big differences between Box2D and Chipmunk2D start to show. Thus, we will explain the addBody function line-by-line:

```
if(isDynamic) {
  var body = new cp.Body(1,cp.momentForBox(1,width,height));
}
else{
  var body = new cp.Body(Infinity,Infinity);
}
```

We have two ways to create a body, irrespective of whether it's static or dynamic. Both use the cp.Body method, whose arguments are the mass and the moment of inertia. The moment of inertia is the mass property of a rigid body that determines the torque needed for a desired angular acceleration about an axis of rotation.

 For more information, visit the Wikipedia article at http://en.wikipedia.org/wiki/Moment_ of_inertia, which explains it very clearly.

When a body is dynamic, I set the mass to 1, but it could be any positive finite number, and the moment of inertia is a result of the calculation of the mass, the width, and the height by the momentForBox method, which does the hard work for us.

So, a box with *mass = 1* will be declared this way:

```
var body = new cp.Body(1,cp.momentForBox(1,width,height));
```

While a box with mass 15 will be declared, replacing 1 with 15 in this way:

```
var body = new cp.Body(15,cp.momentForBox(15,width,height));
```

 Remember, for a dynamic body, the mass can be set to any positive number.

On the other hand, when dealing with static bodies, you must set both the mass and the moment of inertia to an infinite number, which JavaScript represents with infinity.

Once the body is created, you need to give it a position in the space:

```
body.setPos(cp.v(posX,posY));
```

The setPos method places it on the space using pixel coordinates. As you can see, cp.v arguments are the actual pixel coordinates you set when you call the addBody function with no conversions between units of measurement.

If you remember, in the Box2D chapter, you needed to convert meters to pixels. However, Chipmunk2D works directly in pixels.

Now, it's time to add the body to the space:

```
if(isDynamic){
   world.addBody(body);
}
```

The `addBody` method adds a body to the space. You are probably wondering why I am adding the body to it only if it's dynamic. Once a body has been defined as static with infinite mass and a moment of inertia, there's no need to add it to the space unless you plan to move it manually during the game (think about a moving platform, which is not the case with our solid ground), because you will only add its collision shape.

What is a body collision shape? You are about to discover it:

```
var shape = new cp.BoxShape(body, width, height);
```

Pretty much like Box2D, Chipmunk2D works with bodies and shapes, where bodies represent abstract physics entities, and shapes are actual pieces of physics matter attached to bodies. In Box2D, we also use fixtures as glue between a body and a shape while, in Chipmunk2D, this is not necessary: we can directly create a shape and attach it to a body.

Let's create the shape then:

```
var shape = new cp.BoxShape(body, width, height);
shape.setFriction(1);
shape.setElasticity(0);
shape.name=type;
world.addShape(shape);
```

The `cp.BoxShape` method creates the shape, gives a width, height, and a body to attach the shape to `setFriction`, and `setElasticity` defines the shape material, which is referred to as elasticity as Box2D's restitution. I am also giving the shape a name; then the `addShape` method adds the shape to the space.

Now, all these shapes and bodies should be ready to be processed by the Chipmunk2D space, so it's time to see how to run the simulation.

# Updating Chipmunk2D space and using debug draw

To update the Chipmunk2D space, just call the `step` method in the update function:

```
update:function(dt){
  world.step(dt);
}
```

This will make the simulation advance by the `dt` time.

Okay, now run the project and you will see just the background gradient. Did we miss something?

Like Box2D, Chipmunk2D does not draw the space; it simply computes it and leaves us the job of rendering it.

Anyway, to make quick and simple tests, there's a feature called debug draw (also included in Box2D), although I did not show you how to reduce the page count, which allows you to render the space without having actual graphic assets attached to bodies.

Change the `init` function this way:

```
init:function () {
  this._super();
  var backgroundLayer = cc.LayerGradient.create(cc.
color(0xdf,0x9f,0x83,255), cc.color(0xfa,0xf7,0x9f,255));
  this.addChild(backgroundLayer);
  world = new cp.Space();
  world.gravity = cp.v(0, -100);
  var debugDraw = cc.PhysicsDebugNode.create(world);
  debugDraw.setVisible(true);
  this.addChild(debugDraw);
  this.addBody(240,10,480,20,false,"assets/ground.png","ground");
  this.addBody(204,32,24,24,true,"assets/brick1x1.png","destroyable");
  this.addBody(276,32,24,24,true,"assets/brick1x1.png","destroyable");
  this.addBody(240,56,96,24,true,"assets/brick4x1.png","destroyable");
  this.addBody(240,80,48,24,true,"assets/brick2x1.png","solid");
  this.addBody(228,104,72,24,true,"assets/brick3x1.
png","destroyable");
  this.addBody(240,140,96,48,true,"assets/brick4x2.png","solid");
  this.addBody(240,188,24,48,true,"assets/totem.png","totem");
  this.scheduleUpdate();
  cc.eventManager.addListener(touchListener, this);
}
```

These three lines will create a debug draw layer with the `cc.PhysicsDebugNode.create` method, which is later added to the stage.

Run the project now:

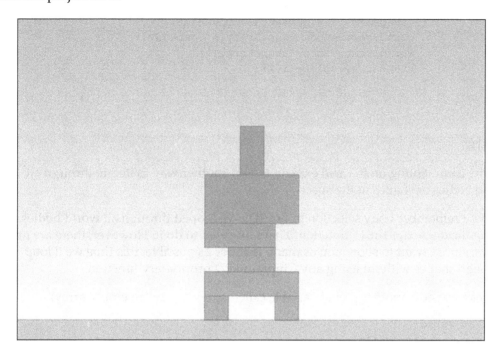

Also, here are our dynamic totem pieces and our static background rendered with debug draw. PhysicsDebug will iterate through the shapes and constraints in space, and draw them with the default color. Now, we can continue adding features to the game and add actual graphic assets once the game is completed. This will save developing time because, if something does not work as it should, then we can use debug draw to see whether Chipmunk2D bodies position-match the graphic assets position.

# Selecting and destroying space bodies

The player must be able to destroy certain bodies: the ones called with the destroyable name by clicking or tapping over them. Thus, this is the complete touchListener declaration:

```
var touchListener = cc.EventListener.create({
  event: cc.EventListener.TOUCH_ONE_BY_ONE,
  onTouchBegan: function (touch, event) {
    for(var i=shapeArray.length-1;i>=0;i--){
```

```
        if(shapeArray[i].pointQuery(cp.v(touch.getLocation().
          x,touch.getLocation().y))!=undefined){
          if(shapeArray[i].name=="destroyable"){
            world.removeBody(shapeArray[i].getBody())
            world.removeShape(shapeArray[i])
            shapeArray.splice(i,1);
          }
        }
      }
    }
  })
```

Before commenting on it, I will explain to you another way to iterate through all these bodies or shapes in the space.

Do you remember body selection in Box2D? We looped through all world bodies using the GetBodyList() function. That's one way to do it. However, there are other ways; since I want to show you as many features as possible, this time we'll loop through shapes without using any Chipmunk2D proprietary function.

We can just add another global variable called shapeArray, an empty array:

```
var world;
var shapeArray=[];
```

Then, in the addBody function, once we add a shape to the space, we append it to shapeArray:

```
addBody: function(posX,posY,width,height,isDynamic,spriteImage,type){
  if(isDynamic){
    var body = new cp.Body(1,cp.momentForBox(1,width,height));
  }
  else{
    var body = new cp.Body(Infinity,Infinity);
  }
  body.setPos(cp.v(posX,posY));
  if(isDynamic){
    world.addBody(body);
  }
  var shape = new cp.BoxShape(body, width, height);
  shape.setFriction(1);
  shape.setElasticity(0);
  shape.name=type;
  world.addShape(shape);
  shapeArray.push(shape);
}
```

Once we have all the shapes in `shapeArray`, it's easy to loop through them and see whether the clicked or touched point is inside one of them thanks to `pointQuery`, whose argument is a vector with stage coordinates. If it does not return `undefined`, it means the point is inside the given shape.

Then, the `removeBody` and `removeShape` space's methods delete the shape and the body, respectively. Remember to manually splice `shapeArray` when you remove something.

Want to see whether this works? Just run the project and click on a destroyable brick:

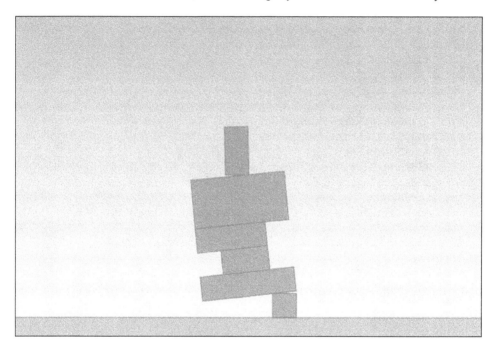

Watch out! It's falling bricks!

This reminds me of two things. First, this is not the best way to solve the level. Second, we have to detect when the idol hits the ground.

# Checking for collisions among bodies

In the previous chapter, to check for collision, we iterated through idol contact points to see when it hit the ground.

Both Box2D and Chipmunk2D have more interesting ways to check for collisions, as they handle collision listeners.

Add the highlighted line to the `init` function:

```
init:function () {
  this._super();
  var backgroundLayer = cc.LayerGradient.create(cc.
color(0xdf,0x9f,0x83,255), cc.color(0xfa,0xf7,0x9f,255));
  this.addChild(backgroundLayer);
  world = new cp.Space();
  world.gravity = cp.v(0, -100);
  this._debugNode = cc.PhysicsDebugNode.create(world);
  this._debugNode.setVisible( true );
  this.addChild( this._debugNode );
  this.scheduleUpdate();
  this.addBody(240,10,480,20,false,"assets/ground.png","ground");
  this.addBody(204,32,24,24,true,"assets/brick1x1.png",
"destroyable");
  this.addBody(276,32,24,24,true,"assets/brick1x1.png",
"destroyable");
  this.addBody(240,56,96,24,true,"assets/brick4x1.png",
"destroyable");
  this.addBody(240,80,48,24,true,"assets/brick2x1.png","solid");
  this.addBody(228,104,72,24,true,"assets/brick3x1.png",
"destroyable");
  this.addBody(240,140,96,48,true,"assets/brick4x2.png","solid");
  this.addBody(240,188,24,48,true,"assets/totem.png","totem");
  cc.eventManager.addListener(touchListener, this);
  world.setDefaultCollisionHandler
  (this.collisionBegin,null,null,null);
}
```

With just one single line, we entered the world of collision listeners. The different types of listeners that can be used are as follows:

- `setDefaultCollisionHandler`: This method will call four functions each time a collision will be updated. In Chipmunk2D as well as in Box2D, a collision has four states:

    ° `begin`: This method defines the time the script realizes that two shapes are touching.

○   preSolve: This method is called just before solving the collision. To solve a collision means to update shapes and bodies according to the collision itself.

○   postSolve: This method is called just after solving the collision.

○   separate: This method is called when the collision ceases to exist—that is, these two shapes are no longer in touch.

We just need to check when the collision begins; that's why I am passing collisionBegin as the first argument, leaving other arguments to null. The collisionBegin function is very simple:

```
collisionBegin : function (arbiter, space ) {
  if((arbiter.a.name=="totem" && arbiter.b.name=="ground") ||
(arbiter.b.name=="totem" && arbiter.a.name=="ground")){
    console.log("Oh no!!!!");
  }
  return true;
}
```

I am just checking whether the first shape: arbiter.a is called totem, and the second shape: arbiter.b is called ground or vice versa to output a console message.

You also have to return true, or the collision will be ignored.

Run the project, and when the totem touches the ground this way:

You will see this:

**Oh no!!!!**

Finally, we completed all the game mechanics of our Totem Destroyer prototype. We just have to add our graphic assets to the game.

Did you notice? We are completing a project by adding graphic assets whereas, in the previous chapter, we started by adding them. This is one of the things I love about programming. Your choices are unlimited.

# Using your own graphic assets

Just as in the previous chapter, we will add graphics when we add a body, then update their position and rotation according to its body position and rotation.

First, update the addBody function:

```
addBody: function
  (posX,posY,width,height,isDynamic,spriteImage,type){
  if(isDynamic){
    var body = new cp.Body(1,cp.momentForBox(1,width,height));
  }
  else{
    var body = new cp.Body(Infinity,Infinity);
  }
  body.setPos(cp.v(posX,posY));
  var bodySprite = cc.Sprite.create(spriteImage);
  gameLayer.addChild(bodySprite,0);
  bodySprite.setPosition(posX,posY);
  if(isDynamic){
    world.addBody(body);
  }
  var shape = new cp.BoxShape(body, width, height);
  shape.setFriction(1);
  shape.setElasticity(0);
  shape.name=type;
  shape.image=bodySprite;
  world.addShape(shape);
  shapeArray.push(shape);
}
```

This works in the same way as we saw with Box2D: a sprite is added to the game and is saved in a custom shape attribute—in this case, `image`.

To update the sprite's position in the `update` function, we need to loop through all shapes:

```
update:function(dt){
  world.step(dt);
  for(var i=shapeArray.length-1;i>=0;i--){
    shapeArray[i].image.x=shapeArray[i].body.p.x
    shapeArray[i].image.y=shapeArray[i].body.p.y
    var angle = Math.atan2(-shapeArray[i].body.rot.y,shapeArray[i].
body.rot.x);
    shapeArray[i].image.rotation= angle*57.2957795;
  }
}
```

We loop through our custom variable, `shapeArray`, and update each shape image according to its body position and rotation. While it's very easy to get a body position with the `p` property, Chipmunk2D does not return a body rotation in degrees or radians, but with a vector; you can get its position with the `rot` property. That's why I am using the `atan2` method to get an angle from a vector; then I multiply it by `57.2957795` to turn radians into degrees.

Also, don't forget to manually remove a sprite when you remove its body:

```
var touchListener = cc.EventListener.create({
  event: cc.EventListener.TOUCH_ONE_BY_ONE,
  onTouchBegan: function (touch, event) {
    for(var i=shapeArray.length-1;i>=0;i--){
      if(shapeArray[i].pointQuery(cp.v(touch.getLocation().
        x,touch.getLocation().y))!=undefined){
        if(shapeArray[i].name=="destroyable"){
          gameLayer.removeChild(shapeArray[i].image);
          world.removeBody(shapeArray[i].getBody())
          world.removeShape(shapeArray[i])
          shapeArray.splice(i,1);
        }
      }
    }
  }
})
```

Run the project and see your custom graphics in action:

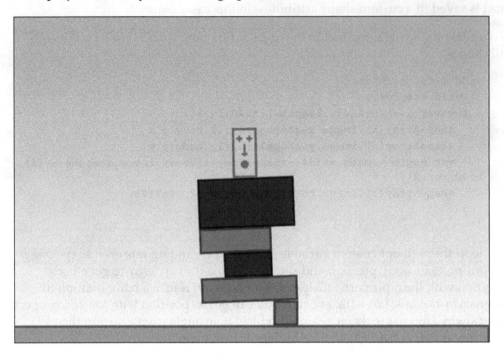

At this time, you can remove debug draw graphics; this leaves you with the same game made with two different physics engines.

# Summary

Let me congratulate you; you not only made a Totem Destroyer game, but you were also able to make it using two different physics engines. Not all developers out there are able to do it. Now, add to the game the same improvement you added to the Box2D game because you improved the game, didn't you? Let's start the last chapter, where you will create a blockbuster game in a matter of minutes.

# 9
# Creating Your Own Blockbuster Game – A Complete Match 3 Game

This is the last chapter of this book, and I really hope you have enjoyed reading it as much as I enjoyed writing it. When I drafted the initial outline for this book, I planned to dedicate the last chapter to a Match 3 game such as Candy Crush Saga or Farm Heroes Saga.

I then realized that there are tons of tutorials about these games available around the Web. Hence, I decided to show y'all something new, the engine of the Dungeon Raid game (available at `https://itunes.apple.com/us/app/dungeon-raid/id403090531`), which I adapted to create Globez (available at `http://www.mindjolt.com/globez.html`), a game that has been played millions of times.

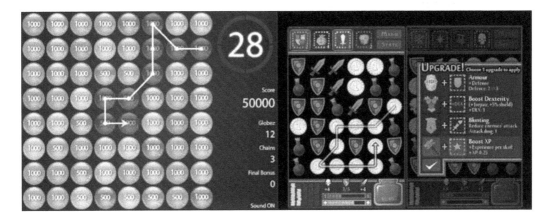

During the making of this game, you will not only use most of the concepts described in this book in the creation of a real game engine, but you will also learn the bare bones of the Cocos2d-JS drawing API.

Follow the steps carefully; this is a complete game engine, and there's a lot to do.

# Setting up the game

Since it's a basic game with no physics, we don't need to include external libraries; so, `project.json` returns to its original content:

```
{
    "debugMode" : 0,
    "showFPS" : false,
    "frameRate" : 60,
    "id" : "gameCanvas",
    "renderMode" : 0,
    "engineDir":"cocos2d-html5/",

    "modules" : ["cocos2d"],

    "jsList" : [
    "src/loadassets.js",
    "src/gamescript.js"
    ]
}
```

Also, the content of `main.js` is basically the same as always:

```
cc.game.onStart = function(){
  var screenSize = cc.view.getFrameSize();
  cc.view.setDesignResolutionSize(300, 300, cc.ResolutionPolicy.SHOW_
ALL);
  cc.LoaderScene.preload(gameResources, function () {
    cc.director.runScene(new gameScene());
  }, this);
};
cc.game.run();
```

Just have a look at the resolution: 300x300 is the main game area. For now, we'll only focus on the main game area, and believe me, you'll have enough to do!

`loadassets.js` is loading a sprite sheet created with **TexturePacker**:

```
var gameResources = [
"assets/globes.png",
"assets/globes.plist",
];
```

`globes.png` is just one single file with all colored globes:

And `globes.plist` defines various images this way, with each color name assigned the `key` node. For example:

```
<key>purple</key>
<dict>
  <key>frame</key>
  <string>{{2,2},{46,46}}</string>
  <key>offset</key>
  <string>{0,0}</string>
  <key>rotated</key>
  <false/>
  <key>sourceColorRect</key>
  <string>{{2,2},{46,46}}</string>
  <key>sourceSize</key>
  <string>{50,50}</string>
</dict>
```

Now that we are done with the settings, we can start coding the game itself.

# Creating the board

The first thing we'll do is create the board in `gamescript.js` on which we'll be playing the game. Trying to make the engine as customizable as we can, we'll start with some global variables. Changing most of them will result in a quick gameplay change. It is shown as follows:

```
var fieldSize = 6;
var tileTypes = ["red", "green", "blue", "grey", "yellow"];
var tileSize = 50;
var tileArray = [];
var globezLayer;
```

- `fieldSize`: This variable is the width and height of the field size, in tiles. This means we will play on a 6 x 6 tile field.

- `tileTypes`: This is an array with the keys of the sprites defined in the `globes.plist` file. I used only five different kinds of globez because I like the game to offer the opportunity to make big combos. You can choose how many colors you want; just keep in mind the more the colors in the game, the harder the gameplay.

- `tileSize`: This variable is the size of a tile, in pixels.
- `tileArray`: This is the array that will contain all globez objects.
- `globezLayer`: This variable will be the layer where globez tiles will be placed.

The `gameScene` definition does not change:

```
var gameScene = cc.Scene.extend({
  onEnter:function () {
    this._super();
    gameLayer = new game();
    gameLayer.init();
    this.addChild(gameLayer);
  }
});
```

Let's have a look at the game definition, the core of the script:

```
var game = cc.Layer.extend({
  init:function () {
    this._super();
    cc.spriteFrameCache.addSpriteFrames
      ("assets/globes.plist", "assets/globes.png");
    var backgroundLayer = cc.LayerGradient.create(cc.
color(0x00,0x22,0x22,255), cc.color(0x22,0x00,0x44,255));
    this.addChild(backgroundLayer);
    globezLayer = cc.Layer.create();
    // new cc.layer() can also be used
    this.addChild(globezLayer)
    this.createLevel();
  },
  createLevel: function(){
    // do something
  }
});
```

There's nothing new here; we load the sprite sheet, create and place a background layer, create and place the layer that will contain all globez, and call the `createLevel` function.

Let's add globe creation to `createLevel`:

```
createLevel: function(){
  for(var i = 0; i < fieldSize; i ++){
    tileArray[i] = [];
    for(var j = 0;j < fieldSize; j ++){
      this.addTile(i, j);
```

```
      }
    }
  },
  addTile:function(row,col){
    // do something
  }
```

Here we are just building a two-dimensional array called `tileArray` according to the `fieldSize` number of entries. Given the *i* and *j* values, the `addTile` function causes the final creation of the tile, which accepts the row and the column of such a tile in the game field.

Let's look at `addTile` to know how to set up a game field:

```
addTile:function(row,col){
  var randomTile = Math.floor(Math.random()*tileTypes.length);
  var spriteFrame = cc.spriteFrameCache.getSpriteFrame(tileTypes[rand
omTile]);
  var sprite = cc.Sprite.createWithSpriteFrame(spriteFrame);
  // new cc.Sprite(spriteFrame) can also be used
  sprite.val = randomTile;
  sprite.picked = false;
  globezLayer.addChild(sprite,0);
  sprite.setPosition
    (col*tileSize+tileSize/2,row*tileSize+tileSize/2);
  tileArray[row][col] = sprite;
}
```

At this point of time, you can test the project and see what happens:

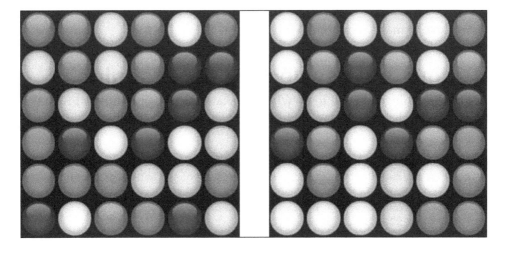

Did you notice? Every time you run the game, you get a different, random game field.

Having a look at the `addTile` function will let you understand what happened:

```
var randomTile = Math.floor(Math.random()*tileTypes.length);
```

First, a random number between zero and the number of allowed tile types minus one is generated. In this case, it is from zero to five.

```
var spriteFrame = cc.spriteFrameCache.getSpriteFrame(tileTypes[random
Tile]);
```

From the sprite sheet, we will pick the sprite with the same key as `tileTypes[randomTile]`:

```
var sprite = cc.Sprite.createWithSpriteFrame(spriteFrame);
```

Finally, the sprite is created starting from its assigned frame:

```
sprite.val = randomTile;
sprite.picked = false;
```

I added two custom attributes to our sprite:

- `val`: This variable represents the value of the tile as defined by the `randomTile` variable
- `picked`: This is a Boolean variable that says whether the tile has currently been picked by the players

Then, the sprite is added to the `globezLayer` layer:

```
globezLayer.addChild(sprite,0);
```

Now, we have to make something with all these globez.

# Selecting and deselecting the first globe

What's the first thing we need to do when we want the player to interact with the game? Yes, add a listener. We will add it to the game's `init` function:

```
init:function () {
  this._super();
  cc.spriteFrameCache.addSpriteFrames("assets/globes.plist", "assets/
globes.png");
  var backgroundLayer = cc.LayerGradient.create(cc.
color(0x00,0x22,0x22,255), cc.color(0x22,0x00,0x44,255));
```

```
    this.addChild(backgroundLayer);
    globezLayer = cc.Layer.create();
    this.addChild(globezLayer)
    this.createLevel();
    cc.eventManager.addListener(touchListener, this);
  }
```

These are all concepts you have already met; I am just putting them together in order to create a game. So, you should know by now that we are going to declare `touchListener`; but first, let me add two more global variables to keep track of all the tiles I am going to select and the color I select:

```
var fieldSize = 6;
var tileTypes = ["red","green","blue","grey","yellow"];
var tileSize = 50;
var tileArray = [];
var globezLayer;
var startColor = null;
var visitedTiles = [];
```

`visitedTiles` is the array that will store the tiles once they have been picked up by the player, while `startColor` is the color of the first tile selected. We start with `null` as no color has been selected.

Now, let's move to the `touchListener` creation:

```
var touchListener = cc.EventListener.create({
  event: cc.EventListener.MOUSE,
  onMouseDown: function (event) {
    var pickedRow = Math.floor(event._y / tileSize);
    var pickedCol = Math.floor(event._x / tileSize);
    tileArray[pickedRow][pickedCol].setOpacity(128);
    tileArray[pickedRow][pickedCol].picked = true;
    startColor = tileArray[pickedRow][pickedCol].val;
    visitedTiles.push({
      row: pickedRow,
      col: pickedCol
    });
  },
  onMouseUp: function(event){
    startColor=null;
    for(i = 0; i < visitedTiles.length; i ++){
      tileArray[visitedTiles[i].row][visitedTiles[i].col].
setOpacity(255);
```

```
        tileArray[visitedTiles[i].row][visitedTiles[i].col].
    picked=false;
        }
    }
});
```

It seems a lot of code but don't worry; it's really easy. Check the following line of code:

```
event: cc.EventListener.MOUSE
```

This time, we will play with the mouse but, obviously, you can use touch if you want. Let's say you should be able to use both ways to control the game. Using the mouse, we have to deal with two events, onMouseDown and onMouseUp:

```
onMouseDown: function (event) {
    var pickedRow = Math.floor(event._y / tileSize);
    var pickedCol = Math.floor(event._x / tileSize);
    tileArray[pickedRow][pickedCol].setOpacity(128);
    tileArray[pickedRow][pickedCol].picked = true;
    startColor = tileArray[pickedRow][pickedCol].val;
    visitedTiles.push({
        row: pickedRow,
        col: pickedCol
    });
}
```

When the mouse is pressed, the pickedRow and pickedCol variables take the index of the row and column picked by the mouse according to click coordinates and tileSize. Once I know the row and column of the globe I picked, I can make it semitransparent by setting its opacity to 128 — remember that opacity ranges from 0 to 255 in Cocos2d-JS with the setOpacity method. Also, I set the globe picked value to true because I actually picked it up, and since it's the first globe I am picking, I also need to set startColor to the globe color. From now on, we will only have to pick globez with the same color.

Last but not least, we need to update the visitedTiles array with the newly picked globe — in this case, it's added as an object.

At the moment, onMouseUp is quite simple, although it will become the most complicated function in the whole game. It is as follows:

```
onMouseUp: function(event){
  startColor=null;
  for(i = 0; i < visitedTiles.length; i ++){
    tileArray[visitedTiles[i].row][visitedTiles[i].col].
      setOpacity(255);
    tileArray[visitedTiles[i].row][visitedTiles[i].col].
      picked=false;
  }
  visitedTiles = [];
}
```

There isn't much to say; once the player releases the mouse, the startColor method needs to be reset to null and each globe in the visitedTiles array must be set to fully opaque, with the picked attribute set to false. With an empty visitedTiles array, we are ready to wait for the next player choice.

Test the game and try to pick and release a globe:

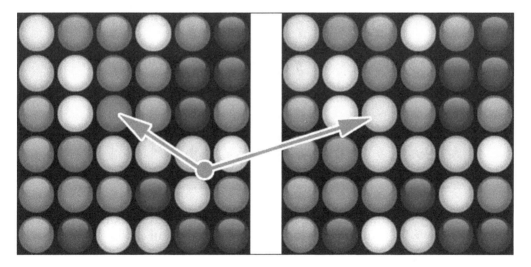

As you can see, when you pick a globe, it turns semitransparent. When you release it, it returns fully opaque.

Let's make our first chain.

# Making globez chains

The gameplay is simple: you have to connect as many globez you can, horizontally, vertically, or diagonally. And you can also backtrack.

Let's see how to connect globez. First, though, let me introduce you to a variable that will be very important in all your draw-to-match games: `tolerance`. Check the following code snippet:

```
var fieldSize = 6;
var tileTypes = ["red","green","blue","grey","yellow"];
var tileSize = 50;
var tileArray = [];
var globezLayer;
var visitedTiles = [];
var startColor = null;
var tolerance = 400;
```

Have a look at the following screenshot:

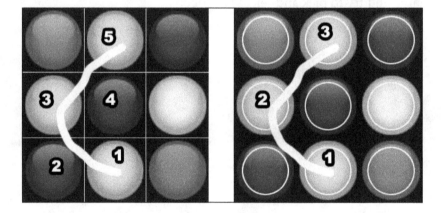

Let's say the player wants to connect the three green globez, from bottom to top. When you draw with your finger on a small surface, say, your mobile phone, maybe in a train, you aren't this precise. So, on the left side, we can see what will happen if we detect player movement in a tile-based environment. The not-that-precise drawing would touch five different globez, resulting in an illegal move, which is frustrating. On the right side, using a tolerance, we only detect a player movement when next to the center of the tile. See the difference? The player only touches three globez, performing a legal move as required.

I called the square of the distance from the center — the radius of the inner white circles — `tolerance`, and in this case, I set it to *20 pixels * 20 pixels = 400*.

We can say we have a legal move when:

- We are inside a tolerance area
- The current globe hasn't already been picked — the `picked` attribute is `false`
- The current globe is adjacent to the last picked globe
- The current globe has the same color as the first picked globe

Translated into Cocos2d-JS, this means the `onMouseMove` function will contain:

```
onMouseMove: function(event){
  if(startColor!=null){
    var currentRow = Math.floor(event._y / tileSize);
    var currentCol = Math.floor(event._x / tileSize);
    var centerX = currentCol * tileSize + tileSize / 2;
    var centerY = currentRow * tileSize + tileSize / 2;
    var distX = event._x - centerX;
    var distY = event._y - centerY;
    if(distX * distX + distY * distY < tolerance){
      if(!tileArray[currentRow][currentCol].picked){
        if(Math.abs(currentRow - visitedTiles[visitedTiles.
          length - 1].row) <= 1 && Math.abs(currentCol -
          visitedTiles[visitedTiles.length -1].col) <= 1){
          if(tileArray[currentRow][currentCol].val==startColor){
            tileArray[currentRow][currentCol].setOpacity(128);
            tileArray[currentRow][currentCol].picked=true;
            visitedTiles.push({
              row:currentRow,
              col:currentCol
            });
          }
        }
      }
    }
  }
}
```

It seems a lot of code but it's just the representation of the four conditions mentioned earlier. I would like to point out the following line to you:

```
if(distX * distX + distY * distY < tolerance){ … }
```

Here, I am applying the **Pythagorean Theorem** without using square roots, to save CPU time.

Test the script, and see what happens:

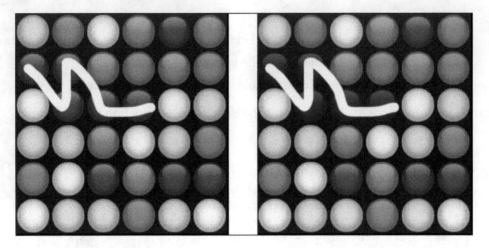

You are now able to select globez even if your drawing is a bit imprecise. Now, what if you change your mind and want to backtrack to try another route?

# Backtracking

You can backtrack your selection when you move your mouse back to the second last globe. In this case, the last globe is removed from the `visitedTiles` array and both the `picked` attribute and the opacity are turned back to their default values: `true` and `255`, respectively.

To check for backtrack, you must check whether:

- We are inside a tolerance area
- The current globe has already been picked — the `picked` attribute is `true`
- The current globe is the second last entry in the `visitedTiles` array

This is just a minor change in the `onMouseMove` code:

```
onMouseMove: function(event){
  if(startColor!=null){
    // same as before
    if(distX * distX + distY * distY < tolerance){
      if(!tileArray[currentRow][currentCol].picked){
        // same as before
      }
      else{
```

```
        if(visitedTiles.length>=2 && currentRow ==
visitedTiles[visitedTiles.length - 2].row && currentCol ==
visitedTiles[visitedTiles.length - 2].col){
            tileArray[visitedTiles[visitedTiles.length - 1].row]
[visitedTiles[visitedTiles.length - 1].col].setOpacity(255);
            tileArray[visitedTiles[visitedTiles.length - 1].row]
[visitedTiles[visitedTiles.length - 1].col].picked=false;
            visitedTiles.pop();
        }
    }
  }
 }
}
```

Test your game now, and try to backtrack. See the following screenshot:

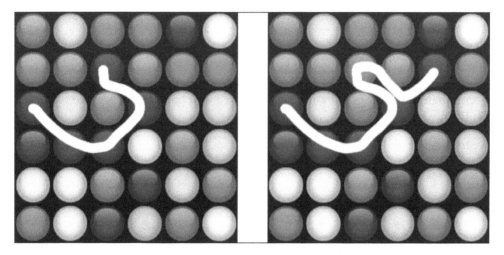

Do you see this? Now, you can change your mind and take another route.

Take a short break because it's not over yet, although we managed to completely handle player movements.

# Removing globez

An ancient proverb says, *it's not a match game if you can't remove items*. And, it's right! Once you select the globez, you must be able to remove them once you release the mouse.

Removing globez is very easy: once you know the `visitedTiles` array has at least three items, just remove those items from the stage and from the `tileArray` array.

Change onMouseUp this way:

```
onMouseUp: function(event){
    startColor=null;
    for(i = 0; i < visitedTiles.length; i ++){
        if(visitedTiles.length<3){
            tileArray[visitedTiles[i].row][visitedTiles[i].col].
setOpacity(255);
            tileArray[visitedTiles[i].row][visitedTiles[i].col].
picked=false;
        }
        else{
            globezLayer.removeChild
                (tileArray[visitedTiles[i].row][visitedTiles[i].col]);
            tileArray[visitedTiles[i].row][visitedTiles[i].col]=null;
        }
    }
    visitedTiles = [];
}
```

Setting removed globez with `null` in the `tileArray` array after having physically removed them from the stage with `removeChild` will be useful when we want to replenish the board.

Now, try the game:

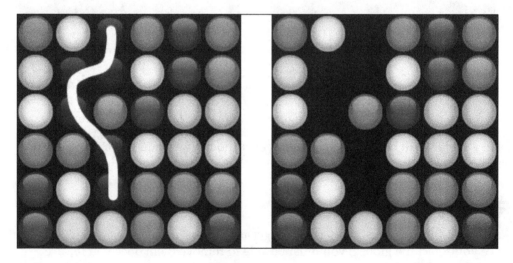

Did you see? We removed the globez. Now, the game is complete. Wait. No. Once you remove the globez, some globez have to fall down and more globez have to appear from the top of the screen to refill the stage. We will make them fall down gently using a tween.

# Making the globez fall down

Once you remove the globez, you will need to check whether there are globez with empty spaces below them, and make them fall down accordingly.

Remember, unlike most other languages, Cocos2d-JS sets the origin (0,0) coordinate at the bottom left of the stage, so the lowest row is row zero.

We need to heavily edit `onMouseUp`:

```
onMouseUp: function(event){
  startColor=null;
  for(i = 0; i < visitedTiles.length; i ++){
    if(visitedTiles.length<3){
      tileArray[visitedTiles[i].row][visitedTiles[i].col].
setOpacity(255);
      tileArray[visitedTiles[i].row][visitedTiles[i].col].
picked=false;
    }
    else{
      globezLayer.removeChild(tileArray[visitedTiles[i].row]
[visitedTiles[i].col]);
      tileArray[visitedTiles[i].row][visitedTiles[i].col]=null;
    }
  }
  if(visitedTiles.length>=3){
    for(i = 1; i < fieldSize; i ++){
      for(j = 0; j < fieldSize; j ++){
        if(tileArray[i][j] != null){
          var holesBelow = 0;
          for(var k = i - 1; k >= 0; k --){
            if(tileArray[k][j] == null){
              holesBelow++;
            }
          }
          if(holesBelow>0){
            var moveAction = cc.MoveTo.create(0.5, new
cc.Point(tileArray[i][j].x,tileArray[i][j].y-holesBelow*tileSize));
```

```
        // cc,moveTo() can also be used
        tileArray[i] [j].runAction(moveAction);
        tileArray[i - holesBelow] [j] = tileArray[i] [j];
        tileArray[i] [j] = null;
      }
    }
  }
}
visitedTiles = [];
}
```

Run the script and see what happens:

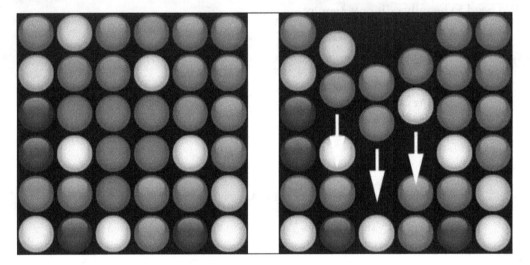

Once green globez have been removed, the upper globez fall down.

Let's analyze the code a little:

```
if(visitedTiles.length>=3){
```

Everything depends on whether we selected more than three globez. Otherwise, no globez will be removed, and there will be no need to check for empty spaces:

```
for(i = 1; i < fieldSize; i ++){
```

We start looping through all rows starting from 1 — the next-to-bottomt row — to row `fieldsize`-1, which is the topmost row.

```
for(j = 0; j < fieldSize; j ++){
```

We do the same thing for the columns but, this time, we scan them.

```
if(tileArray[i][j] != null){
```

If in the given position we have a globe, it's time to count how many empty spaces we have below it.

```
var holesBelow = 0;
```

The `holesBelow` variable will keep track of the empty spaces below a globe.

```
for(var k = i - 1; k >= 0; k --){
```

Starting from the current row and going down to the first, we have to count the empty spaces.

```
if(tileArray[k][j] == null){
```

We find an empty space when its `tileArray` value is null.

```
holesBelow++;
```

And, in this case, we increment the `holesBelow` variable:

```
if(holesBelow>0){
```

Once the loop has finished, we check whether there were holes below:

```
var moveAction = cc.MoveTo.create(0.5, new cc.Point(tileArray[i]
[j].x,tileArray[i][j].y-holesBelow*tileSize));
tileArray[i][j].runAction(moveAction);
```

Then, move the globe accordingly.

```
tileArray[i - holesBelow][j] = tileArray[i][j];
tileArray[i][j] = null;
```

Finally, we can update `tileArray` to register the new position of the globe.

Now that we managed to make the globez fall down, there is just one more thing to do — create new globes to fill the stage again.

# Creating new globez

Creating new globez shares the same concept as making the globez fall. For each column, we count the number of empty places; this number is the number of globez we have to create.

In order to create a smooth appearance, each globe will be created outside the top of the stage and an animation tween will place it in its right place.

This is the last time we need to modify onMouseUp, promise!

```
onMouseUp: function(event){
  // same as before
  if(visitedTiles.length>=3){
    // same as before
    for(i = 0; i < fieldSize; i ++){
      for(j = fieldSize-1; j>=0; j --){
        if(tileArray[j][i] != null){
          break;
        }
      }
      var missingGlobes = fieldSize-1-j;
      if(missingGlobes>0){
        for(j=0;j<missingGlobes;j++){
          this.fallTile(fieldSize-j-1,i,missingGlobes-j)
        }
      }
    }
  }
  visitedTiles = [];
}
```

This is the part needed to scan for empty spaces and call the fallTile method to create a new tile with the destination row, destination column, and falling height. We use the falling height to create a smooth tween to the globe's final position.

Here's the definition for fallTile:

```
fallTile:function(row,col,height){
  var randomTile = Math.floor(Math.random()*tileTypes.length);
  var spriteFrame = cc.spriteFrameCache.
    getSpriteFrame(tileTypes[randomTile]);
  var sprite = cc.Sprite.createWithSpriteFrame(spriteFrame);
  sprite.val = randomTile;
  sprite.picked = false;
```

```
    globezLayer.addChild(sprite,0);
    sprite.setPosition
        (col*tileSize+tileSize/2,(fieldSize+height)*tileSize);
    var moveAction = cc.MoveTo.create(0.5, new cc.Point(col*tileSize+til
eSize/2,row*tileSize+tileSize/2));
    sprite.runAction(moveAction);
    tileArray[row][col] = sprite;
}
```

It's really similar to the `addTile` method created several pages ago—it was a long journey, wasn't it? And finally Globez is made:

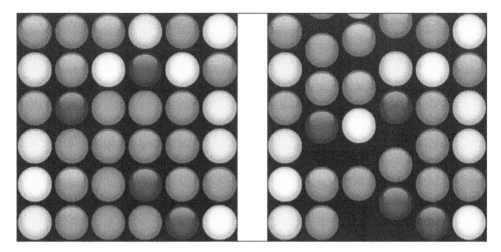

Once you remove some globez, new ones will fall down from the top.

# Bonus – using the drawing API for a visual feedback

As promised, we will use the drawing API to provide a visual feedback of the path we are drawing with the mouse.

First, let's create a new global variable to store the layer where we will draw the player movement. It's called `arrowsLayer`:

```
var fieldSize = 6;
var tileTypes = ["red","green","blue","grey","yellow"];
var tileSize = 50;
var tileArray = [];
var globezLayer;
```

```
var arrowsLayer;
var visitedTiles = [];
var startColor = null;
var tolerance = 400;
```

We will create and add `arrowLayer` after `globezLayer` in the `init` function:

```
init:function () {
  this._super();
  cc.spriteFrameCache.addSpriteFrames("assets/globes.plist", "assets/
globes.png");
  var backgroundLayer = cc.LayerGradient.create(cc.
color(0x00,0x22,0x22,255), cc.color(0x22,0x00,0x44,255));
  this.addChild(backgroundLayer);
  globezLayer = cc.Layer.create();
  this.addChild(globezLayer)
  arrowsLayer = cc.DrawNode.create();
  // new cc.DrawNode() can also be used
  this.addChild(arrowsLayer);
  this.createLevel();
  cc.eventManager.addListener(touchListener, this);
}
```

The entity we can draw in is `DrawNode`.

No matter what happens, when we release the mouse, we will clear the draw area using the `clear` method:

```
onMouseUp: function(event){
  arrowsLayer.clear();
  // same as before
}
```

Now, we know how to clear a draw node and we have to see how to draw lines in it. Add a new method call when the player performs a legal move, no matter whether you're selecting a new globe or backtracking:

```
onMouseMove: function(event){
  if(startColor!=null){
    // same as before
    if(distX * distX + distY * distY < tolerance){
      // same as before
      this.drawPath();
    }
  }
}
```

And now the only thing to do is the creation of `touchListener` listener's `drawPath` method:

```
drawPath:function(){
  arrowsLayer.clear();
  if(visitedTiles.length>0){
    for(var i=1;i<visitedTiles.length;i++){
      arrowsLayer.drawSegment(new cc.Point
        (visitedTiles[i-1].col*tileSize+tileSize/2,
        visitedTiles[i-1].row*tileSize+tileSize/2),
        new cc.Point(visitedTiles[i].col*tileSize+tileSize/2,
        visitedTiles[i].row*tileSize+tileSize/2), 4,
        cc.color(255, 255, 255, 255));
    }
  }
}
```

As you can see, I loop through the `visitedTiles` array and use the `drawSegment` method to draw a segment from the first `cc.Point` argument to the second.

Finally, your game is completed. For real!!

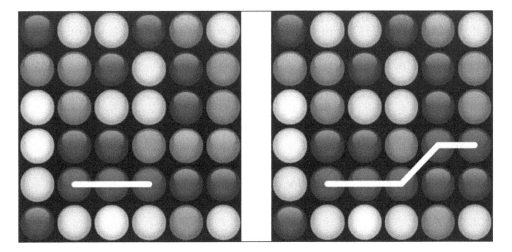

Look how you can draw lines with the mouse, connecting the various globez you selected.

# Where to go now

Normally, each chapter ends with a summary heading; anyway, this time I don't think you need a summary. I mean, you made several games, from a Concentration to Sokoban, from an endless runner to Globez.

First, I want to thank you for reading the entire book, and I hope you enjoyed reading it as much as I enjoyed writing it.

Although you created several games, this is just the beginning of a long journey into cross-platform game development.

First, you should complete the game by adding sounds, a scoring system, and some other features I am sure you know how to add, now that you are reading these final pages.

Then, I just want to point you to three sites you may find useful if you want to dive into cross-platform HTML5 development.

# Protect your code

As your games were written in JavaScript, anyone can look at your code simply by directly looking at the HTML of your pages. There are several tools to obfuscate your code to make it unreadable—or at least to make life really hard for code lurkers. I selected two of them:

1. **Javascript Obfuscator** (`http://javascriptobfuscator.com/`): This is an online free tool to obfuscate your code; just copy-and-paste your code or upload small files and it does the hard work for you.

2. **JScrambler** (`https://jscrambler.com`): This is the one I currently use and recommend. This allows you a lot of obfuscation levels, mobile gaming optimizations, site-locking, expiration dates, and many more. Just drag-and-drop your project and download the protected version.

# Port your game on mobile devices as a native app

Once your game is running on each browser, you may be tempted to convert it into a native mobile app to try to conquer new markets. There are three awesome tools that allow you to create mobile apps starting from HTML, CSS, and JavaScript:

1. Cocos2D proprietary JSB API (`http://www.cocos2d-x.org/wiki/Basic_usage_of_JSB_API`): This is the official API to bind C++ to JavaScript. Starting from a Cocos2d-iphone or Cocos2d-x project, you can have all graphics, rendering, and physics code running natively with the game logic running JavaScript.

2. **PhoneGap** (`http://phonegap.com/`): This application works both from your computer using native SDKs and from the cloud. PhoneGap compiles your HTML5 games, creating native apps ready to be published in markets such as Apple App Store. I used it to create the iOS version of BWBan (`https://itunes.apple.com/us/app/bwban/id783208885?mt=8`), starting from an HTML5 game.

3. **CocoonJS** (`https://www.ludei.com/cocoonjs/`): This platform provides you with a platform to test, accelerate, deploy, and monetize your HTML5 apps and games on all mobile devices with many interesting features to help you deliver great web products faster.

# Publishing your game

Making games is fun, but having people playing your games is even more fun. Here are the two top gaming portals where you should upload your games to receive plays, ratings, comments, and feedback:

1. **Newgrounds** (`http://www.newgrounds.com/`): This web gaming portal has a collection of the best indie audios, web movies, and games made by developers all around the world.

2. **Kongregate** (`http://www.kongregate.com/`): This is my favorite web gaming portal; it also offers an interesting revenue share.

# Licensing your game

Game publishers are always looking for quality games and are willing to pay you to license them to use and customize your game. Unfortunately, it's not that easy to get in touch with them and get enough attention. Luckily, there's a service that does the hard job for you, showing your game to hundreds of potential buyers:

1. **FGL** (https://www.fgl.com/): This is the industry's leading distribution and monetization services for HTML5, Android, iOS, Unity, and Flash. I got several sponsorships, thanks to FGL. I highly recommend working with them.

# Staying up-to-date

The HTML5 gaming market is a new market changing almost daily. You will need to stay up-to-date to know news and trends. There's one forum I highly recommend:

1. **HTML5GameDevs** (http://www.html5gamedevs.com/): This is the top HTML5 Game Dev forum with articles, game releases, frameworks, demos, videos, tutorials, blog posts, and more.

And obviously, my blog, http://www.emanueleferonato.com/, is updated with almost daily news and tutorials.

Finally, you can refer to the official Cocos2d-JS site, http://www.cocos2d-x.org/wiki/Cocos2d-JS, where you can find all new releases and under-development features.

# Summary

In this last chapter, you created a complete prototype of a Match-3 game using most of the features you learned during the reading of this book. Now, you should be able to create your own games starting from scratch, porting your ideas from pencil and paper to modern web browsers and mobile devices.

# Index

## A

**assets, Concentration game**
  about 27
  title, picking as initial attempt 27-30
**asteroids, Helicopter game**
  adding 47-49
  versus spaceship collision 50, 51
**Audacity**
  URL 74

## B

**background color**
  changing 18, 19
**backtracking 148, 149**
**board**
  creating 139-142
**Box2D**
  about 102
  adding, to project 102, 103
  body, adding 107-112
  collisions among bodies, checking 118, 119
  URL 102
**BWBan**
  URL 57

## C

**cart**
  controlling, virtual pad used 93-96
  controlling, with finger 97, 98
  controlling, with ghost buttons 90-93
**Chipmunk2D engine**
  adding 122

  collisions among bodies, checking 132-134
  physics game 122, 123
**Chipmunk2D space**
  bodies, adding to 125-127
  updating 127-129
**CocoonJS**
  about 159
  URL 159
**Cocos2d-JS**
  about 8
  Cocos Code IDE 8
  project structure 10
  requisites 8, 9
  sounds 73
  URL 9, 160
  working 8
**Cocosban game**
  about 57
  finishing 70, 71
  graphic assets, loading 58-60
  level, building 61-66
  sprite sheets 58
  swipes, detecting 66-70
  texture atlases 58
  TexturePacker 58
**Cocos Code IDE**
  URL 8
**code**
  protecting 158
**Concentration game**
  about 21
  gradient background, adding 24, 25
  multiple instances, creating 22, 23
  Sprite class, extending 25-27
**constraint solver 106**

CreateBody method 110
createLevel function 140
cross-platform games 8
CSS sprites 58

## D

debug draw
  using 127-129
drawing API
  using 155-157
Dungeon Raid
  URL 137

## E

endless runner. *See* Helicopter game
endless scrolling background,
          Helicopter game
  adding 39-42

## F

FGL
  URL 160
first globe
  deselecting 142-145
  selecting 142-145

## G

ghost buttons
  used, for controlling cart 90-93
globez
  connecting 146, 147
  creating 154
  fall down activity 151-153
  removing 149
Globez
  URL 137
Google Chrome 9
gradient background, Concentration game
  adding 24, 25
graphic assets, Cocosban game
  loading 58-60
graphic assets, Totem Destroyer
  using 134-136

graphic resources, Helicopter game
  loading 38, 39
  placing 38, 39

## H

Helicopter game
  about 37
  asteroids, adding 47-50
  asteroid, versus spaceship collision 50, 51
  endless scrolling background, adding 39-42
  graphic resources, loading 38, 39
  graphic resources, placing 38, 39
  invulnerability feature 52, 53
  particles, adding 54-56
  spaceship, adding 42-44
  spaceship, controlling 44-47
  spaceship, preventing to
          fly off screen 53, 54
Hello Cross-World
  about 11-14
  debugMode 13
  engineDir 13
  frameRate 13
  id 13
  jsList 13
  modules 13
  showFPS 13
HTML5GameDevs 160

## I

images
  adding 14-18
  preloading 14-17
  removing 18, 19

## J

Javascript Obfuscator
  URL 158
JavaScript Object Notation (JSON) 10
JSB API
  about 159
  URL 159
JScrambler
  URL 158

## K

Kongregate
  about 159
  URL 159

## L

landscape game, virtual pads
  creating 85-90
  update function, conditions 89
level, Cocosban game
  building 61-66
  cratesArray 65
  playerPosition 65
  playerSprite 65

## M

MAMP
  URL 9
Match 3 game
  backtracking 148
  board, creating 139-142
  drawing API, using for visual feedback 155
  first globe, deselecting 142
  first globe, selecting 142
  globez, connecting 146
  globez, creating 154
  globez fall down activity 151
  globez, removing 149
  licensing 160
  porting, on mobile devices as
      native app 159
  publishing 159
  setting up 138, 139
  updating 160
multiple instances, Concentration game
  creating 22, 23
music
  effects, managing 77-79

## N

Newgrounds
  about 159
  URL 159

## O

onTouchBegan event 95
onTouchEnded event 95
onTouchMoved event 95

## P

particles, Helicopter game
  adding 54, 55
  reference link 54
PhoneGap
  about 159
  URL 159
physics space
  configuring 124, 125
physics world
  configuring 104-106
picture, Concentration game
  displaying 30-33
project structure, Cocos2d-JS
  about 10
  cocos2d-html5 10
  index.html 10
  main.js 10
  project.json 10
PSPad
  URL 8
Pythagorean Theorem 147

## R

RGBA (Red, Green, Blue, Alpha) format 24

## S

score, Concentration game
  adding 34-36
SetAsBox method 109
Sokoban game 57
sounds
  effects, managing 77-79
  getMusicVolume method 79
  Menu.create function 76
  menu, creating 75-77
  preloading 74

selecting 73, 74
setMusicVolume method 79
**space bodies, Chipmunk2D engine**
destroying 129-131
selecting 129-131
**spaceship collision, Helicopter game**
versus asteroids 50, 51
**spaceship, Helicopter game**
adding 42-44
controlling 45-47
preventing, to fly off screen 53, 54
**Sprite class, Concentration game**
extending 25-27
**sprite images, Concentration game**
changing 30
**sprites position**
updating 113-116
**swipes, Cocosban game**
detecting 66-70

# T

**texture atlases** 58
**TexturePacker**
about 138
URL 58
**TextWrangler**
URL 8

**tile-based games** 57
**tiles, Concentration game**
picking, as initial attempt 27-30
shuffling 34-36
**Totem Destroyer**
URL 102

# V

**virtual pads**
about 82-84
cart controlling, ghost buttons used 90-93
cart controlling, with fingers 97, 98
landscape game, creating 85-90
onTouchBegan event 95
onTouchEnded event 95
onTouchMoved event 95
used, for controlling cart 93-96

# W

**WAMP**
URL 9
**world bodies, Box2D engine**
destroying 116-118
selecting 116-118

## Thank you for buying
# Learning Cocos2d-JS Game Development

# About Packt Publishing

Packt, pronounced 'packed', published its first book, *Mastering phpMyAdmin for Effective MySQL Management*, in April 2004, and subsequently continued to specialize in publishing highly focused books on specific technologies and solutions.

Our books and publications share the experiences of your fellow IT professionals in adapting and customizing today's systems, applications, and frameworks. Our solution-based books give you the knowledge and power to customize the software and technologies you're using to get the job done. Packt books are more specific and less general than the IT books you have seen in the past. Our unique business model allows us to bring you more focused information, giving you more of what you need to know, and less of what you don't.

Packt is a modern yet unique publishing company that focuses on producing quality, cutting-edge books for communities of developers, administrators, and newbies alike. For more information, please visit our website at www.packtpub.com.

# About Packt Open Source

In 2010, Packt launched two new brands, Packt Open Source and Packt Enterprise, in order to continue its focus on specialization. This book is part of the Packt Open Source brand, home to books published on software built around open source licenses, and offering information to anybody from advanced developers to budding web designers. The Open Source brand also runs Packt's Open Source Royalty Scheme, by which Packt gives a royalty to each open source project about whose software a book is sold.

# Writing for Packt

We welcome all inquiries from people who are interested in authoring. Book proposals should be sent to author@packtpub.com. If your book idea is still at an early stage and you would like to discuss it first before writing a formal book proposal, then please contact us; one of our commissioning editors will get in touch with you.

We're not just looking for published authors; if you have strong technical skills but no writing experience, our experienced editors can help you develop a writing career, or simply get some additional reward for your expertise.

## Learning Cocos2d-x Game Development

ISBN: 978-1-78398-826-6          Paperback: 266 pages

Learn cross-platform game development with Cocos2d-x

1.  Create a Windows Store account and upload your game for distribution.

2.  Develop a game using Cocos2d-x by going through each stage of game development process step by step.

---

## Cocos2d-x Game Development Essentials

ISBN: 978-1-78398-786-3          Paperback: 136 pages

Create iOS and Android games from scratch using Cocos2d-x

1.  Create and run Cocos2d-x projects on iOS and Android platforms.

2.  Find practical solutions to many real-world game development problems.

2.  Learn the essentials of Cocos2d-x by writing code and following step-by-step instructions.

Please check **www.PacktPub.com** for information on our titles

## Cocos2d-X by Example Beginner's Guide

ISBN: 978-1-78216-734-1          Paperback: 246 pages

Make fun games for any platform using C++, combined with one of the most popular open source frameworks in the world

1. Learn to build multi-device games in simple, easy steps, letting the framework do all the heavy lifting.

2. Spice things up in your games with easy to apply animations, particle effects, and physics simulation.

3. Quickly implement and test your own gameplay ideas, with an eye for optimization and portability.

## Learning iPhone Game Development with Cocos2D 3.0

ISBN: 978-1-78216-014-4          Paperback: 434 pages

Harness the power of Cocos2D to create your own stunning and engaging games for iOS

1. Find practical solutions to many real-world game development problems.

2. Create games from start to finish by writing code and following detailed step-by-step instructions.

3. Full of illustrations and diagrams, practical examples, and tips for deeper understanding of game development in Cocos2D for iPhone.

Please check **www.PacktPub.com** for information on our titles